Measuring
Social Life Feelings

*Improved Methods for Assessing
How People Feel About Society
and Their Place in Society*

Karl F. Schuessler

Measuring
Social Life Feelings

Jossey-Bass Publishers

San Francisco • Washington • London • 1982

MEASURING SOCIAL LIFE FEELINGS
*Improved Methods for Assessing How People Feel About Society
and Their Place in Society*
by Karl F. Schuessler

Copyright © 1982 by: Jossey-Bass Inc., Publishers
433 California Street
San Francisco, California 94104

&

Jossey-Bass Limited
28 Banner Street
London EC1Y 8QE

Library of Congress Cataloging in Publication Data

Schuessler, Karl F.
   Measuring social life feelings.

   Bibliography: p. 167
   Includes index.
   1. Sociology—Research. 2. Sociology—
Methodology. I. Title.
HM51.S352   1982   301'.07'2   82-48063
ISBN 0-87589-548-4

Manufactured in the United States of America

The paper in this book meets the guidelines for
permanence and durability of the Committee on
Production Guidelines for Book Longevity of the
Council on Library Resources.

JACKET DESIGN BY WILLI BAUM

FIRST EDITION

Code 8235

The Jossey-Bass
Social and Behavioral Science Series

Special Adviser
Methodology of Social
and Behavioral Research

DONALD W. FISKE
University of Chicago

Preface

In focusing on the scaling of social life feelings, this book presents twelve social life feeling scales and the method of constructing them. The term *social life feeling* is used to denote a sentiment about the social world or an affect-state that comes from living in that world. "A person born at the bottom has little chance of getting ahead" is a feeling about the social world and the way it works. "I feel good about my job" is a feeling about self that presumably reflects the quality of one's experience on the job. The term is thus used broadly to cover concepts pertaining to both a person's outlook on society (cynical, pessimistic, fatalistic) and her or his frame of mind in society (demoralized, estranged, alienated).

The concept *social life feeling* intends to capture the common meaning of the twelve scales. It is the common denominator; it was adopted in the course of constructing the scales, not beforehand. Starting with a few concepts such as *morale* and *malaise,* we first listed scales that were similar in concept or composition and then searched for a term descriptive of their contents collectively—the content domain. Among other terms, we considered *attitude, opinion, value, frame of mind, outlook on life, philosophy of life.* Each of these in its own way struck us as being too narrow. By comparison, social life feeling seemed broad enough to capture what the items making up the domain had in common—namely, a reference to the quality of social circumstances (for example, The world is a friendly place) or to the quality of one's mental well-being in those social circumstances (for example, I often feel left out). The term may be regarded as a tag for this common element and, by extension, for the general meaning of the twelve scales.

Although the background of this book is sociology, its relevance is not limited to that field. Its contents will be pertinent to specialists on social climates and their effects, to specialists on trends in the quality of subjective well-being, to specialists on cross-national research, and to specialists on civic apathy, among others. Its subject matter will also be pertinent to specialists on social measurement, especially the measurement of subjective phenomena, in either its theoretical aspect, or applied. In addition, teachers may find the book a useful lesson on the topic of scale construction.

Individual chapters are interdependent in the sense that questions arising in one chapter may find their answers in another. For example, the problem of missing data is treated toward the end of the book, but questions on that issue may occur to the reader at the very beginning. The overview of contents, next given, reflects the mutuality of chapters.

Overview of Contents

The arrangement of this book is somewhat unconventional. The twelve social life feeling scales form the book proper; the design and collection of the data form the appendix. This arrangement we supposed would correspond to the interests of the average reader—more interest in the scales as such with a view to using them, less interest in the design of the data set. This reverses the usual sequence of topics—namely, design and sampling first, results and conclusions second.

By this arrangement of materials we do not mean to imply that our scales are free of design effects. On the contrary, they were determined by the content of our data set and the method of its production. We wish merely to note that the scales may be considered in their internal characteristics (for instance, alpha reliability) and external relations (for instance, to education) and also in their possible applications, without ever referring to the details of their construction. However, a critical appreciation of their capabilities and limitations requires familiarity with the content domain, the survey questionnaire, and the survey sample, all described in the Appendixes.

Chapter One states the research problem in a general way and our method of answering it. It also reviews the practice of measuring social life feelings in sociology during the last fifty years or so. In the light of this review, it appears that social life feeling measures had their origin in social problems rather than in social theory. Examples are the problem of low worker morale (job dissatisfaction) and the problem of low civic morale (political alienation).

Chapter Two is a description of the twelve social life feeling scales. For each scale, we give the items it comprises, the keyed response for each item, and the percentage giving the keyed response in the national survey sample; and also the mean score, the standard deviation, alpha reliability, and the Tucker-Lewis reliability coefficient. We comment briefly on differences between scales in these respects, a comparison that anticipates the subject matter of Chapter Seven, scale evaluation.

In Chapter Three we describe the construction of the twelve scales. A nontechnical summary would run something like this: Starting with the responses of the 1,522 adults to 237 social life feeling items, we correlated each item with every other item as a first step in analyzing the pattern of their interrelations; second, we dropped items which were uncorrelated with practically every other item and whose selection for the questionnaire was a miscalculation by that criterion; third, we grouped items by the criterion that items within groupings show substantially more correlation than items across groupings; fourth, we purged these groupings of items whose credentials for membership were unacceptable (by statistical criteria). Our social life feeling scales are the best of the screened groupings.

Chapter Four considers the relation of the twelve social life feeling scales to author scales, topic scales, and subject-class scales. An author scale is a set of items appearing in a previously constructed scale; the five items making up the original Srole Anomia Scale (1956) are a case in point. A topic scale is a set of items considered to be on the same topic; a set of items mentioning or alluding to trust is an example. A subject-class scale is a set of assertions about the same subject, such as a set of assertions about self.

Our purposes in investigating these relations was to determine whether the twelve social life feeling scales were closely correlated with such differently constructed scales and whether such correlations lent support to or called into question our interpretations of what the twelve scales were measuring. We were also concerned with the possibility that scale differences were due not to differences in feelings but rather to the tendency of respondents to give correlated answers to items alike in direction of wording (negative or positive) and subject class (self or others). We hypothesized that these tendencies accounted for the differences between scales or that we had spuriously ascribed to differences in feelings what was actually due to differences in question wording—the greater willingness to endorse a negative statement than to reject a positive; the greater consistency in responding to personal statements than to impersonal.

In Chapter Five we consider the relation of the twelve social life feeling scales to age, race, income, education, and marital status. The method of this chapter is the analysis of variance, or the sigificance of the difference between class means. We ask generally whether differences in social background correspond to differences in social life feeling scores. For example, we consider whether whites and nonwhites differ in their scores.

The suggestion has been made that the relations between social life feeling scores and background factors be represented by a structural model and quantified by econometric methods. Although this suggestion is timely, it presupposes what is presently missing (at least in sociology)—namely, a theory about the relation between social life feelings and social background (family, religion, occupation). In the absence of theory, it is impossible to specify a structural model (set of simultaneous equations); it would be possible to write an arbitrary model and to quantify that, but that would be more a statistical exercise than a serious sociological proposal.

The subject matter of Chapter Six is responding desirably and acquiescing and the relation of these response tendencies to both the twelve social life feeling scales and selected social background factors (age, education, and the like). We begin with a description of five response-set scales, two of our own making, labelled RD16 and A16; and three based on items drawn from three previously constructed scales: Jackson's Social Desirability Scale (1967); Jackson and Messick's Acquiescing Scale (1961); and Marlowe and Crowne's Social Desirability Scale (1960). We then discuss the construction of our own scales (RD16 and A16) in some detail and, though in considerably less detail, the makeup of three short forms. The possible effect of responding desirably and acquiescing on the twelve social life feeling scales is considered, using the partial variance as an index of the magnitude of these effects. We also consider the possibility of using RD16 and A16 (our own response-set scales) as covariates for adjusting content scores for response bias.

Our findings on response sets are by no means conclusive. In any given response, it is extremely difficult to calculate the weight of a response set relative to the weight of the feeling being measured. Our work represents more an approach to the problem than a definitive solution.

Chapter Seven provides an evaluation of the twelve social life feeling scales and a perspective on that evaluation. We undertook to rate each scale as superior, good, or fair. By the highest possible standards, our scales stand relatively low; however, relative to what is possible, they may be near the upper limit. The scales thus point to a common predicament in sociology: one must either make do with scales that are the best possible or do without scales altogether.

We provide appendixes covering five topics: (1) the content domain; (2) questionnaire construction; (3) the sample survey; (4) weighting procedures; and (5) formulas used in this research. Our justification for relegating these topics to the appendixes is their marginal interest for the average reader and their lack of technical novelty.

Acknowledgments

These acknowledgments give little idea of how much I owe to the thought and help of others; they are more a word of thanks than a statement of debt.

The research evolved in discussions with John Cardascia, Daniel J. Duross, David F. Hittle, and Patrik I. Madaras, graduate students in sociology at Indiana University at the time. These same four did the pilot survey and had a hand in analyzing the national survey data. The more elaborate statistics of this volume were largely the work of Edwin Davies, Larry Freshnock, Robert Parker, David Prensky, Michael Wallace, and Peter Oberto, also graduate students at the time. In interpreting the twelve empirical scales, I was aided by Michelle P. Evans's analysis of their face validities and by Robin S. Stryker's careful coverage of related literatures.

In the early stages, Howard Schuman, Charlotte Slider, and Lawrence J. Stricker served as consulting specialists. Along the way, the following gave helpful advice: Duane Alwin, Gerhard Arminger, George Bohrnstedt, Norman Bradburn, Hans-Dieter Klingemann, Melvin Kohn, Karl Ulrich Mayer, Walter Müller, Peter Schmidt, Howard Schuman, Melvin Seeman, and Lawrence J. Stricker. Donald Fiske read the entire manuscript and suggested ways of dropping and adding materials and reordering segments for the sake of a more orderly account.

I am indebted to Janice K. Kennedy as much for her concern with the project's welfare as for her expert secretarial assistance. Eleanor Schloesser was meticulous in typing the final manuscript. I am also indebted to Ruby Gayle James, Dagmar Haas, and Anne Scholfield for their smooth typing of chapters in the rough.

The research was supported by U.S. Public Health Service Grant (MH22294). It was also supported in a variety of ways by Indiana University, especially by Sheldon Stryker, Elton Jackson, and Peter Burke, whose priorities and policies as sociology chairpersons in turn contributed materially to this writing.

Bloomington, Indiana   Karl F. Schuessler
August 1982

Contents

Preface   ix

The Author   xvii

1.   Issues in Measuring People's Social   1
   Life Feelings

2.   Using Agree-Disagree Items to Measure   11
   Feelings

3.   Selecting Statements and Constructing   42
   the Scales

4.   Comparing Social Life Feeling Scales   55
   to Other Measures

5. How Social Background Influences   73
    People's Responses

6. Relation of Scores to the Ways People   88
    Respond to Questions

7. Evaluating the Reliability and Validity   123
    of Social Life Feeling Scales

Appendixes: Design and Collection of Data

A. Constructing the Content Domain   141

B. Questionnaire Construction   144

C. Sampling and Interviewing   152

D. Adjusting the Data   155

E. Statistical Formulas   161

    References   167

    Index   175

The Author

Karl F. Schuessler is Distinguished Professor of Sociology at Indiana University, where he has taught since 1947. He earned his bachelor's degree in history and government at Evansville College in Indiana (1936), his master's degree in social science at the University of Chicago (1939), and his doctoral degree in sociology at Indiana University (1947). He served as instructor at Vanderbilt University before his appointment to the sociology faculty at Indiana University.

Schuessler was editor of the *American Sociological Review*, an official publication of the American Sociological Association (ASA), from 1969 to 1971. He served as editor of *Sociological Methodology*, also an official publication of the ASA, for the 1978, 1979, and 1980 volumes. Schuessler's other publications include *Analyzing Social Data* (with H. Costner, 1971; 3rd ed., 1977); *On Analyzing Crime* (1973), a second edition of the late E. H. Sutherland's papers in criminology; and *Social Policy and Sociology* (with J. Demerath and O. Larsen, 1975); *Statistical Reasoning in Sociology* (with J. H. Mueller and H. Costner, 3rd ed., 1977).

During the last twenty-five years, Schuessler has worked as consultant for the National Science Foundation (NSF), the National Institute of Mental Health (NIMH), the National Research Council (NRC), and the Law Enforcement Assistance Administration (LEAA), among other institutes and agencies. He served as chair of the NIMH Study Section on Training Grants in the Social Sciences. For several years, he was attached to an NRC committee to evaluate the work of poverty institutes; more recently, he was attached to an NRC panel on assessing manpower needs in the behavioral sciences.

In 1963, Schuessler was a research consultant to the Political Science Faculty at Thammasat University, Bangkok, Thailand; the materials developed for use by that faculty and their students were published in book form by the university in 1964. In 1979, he was a guest scholar at the Center for Survey Research, Mannheim, West Germany, and in 1980 he was attached to the Social Science Institute, University of Mannheim. His twelve Social Life Feelings Scales are being translated into German so that they may be administered to a representative sample in West Germany.

Measuring Social Life Feelings

Improved Methods for Assessing How People Feel About Society and Their Place in Society

1

Issues in
Measuring People's
Social Life Feelings

Many scales for measuring social life feelings have appeared in American sociology, but few have been used with any regularity. To what degree do these many scales overlap? Is it possible that a few representative scales might do the work of the many now in existence? This volume intends to throw light on these questions. In it twelve social life feeling scales and the method of their construction are presented. As noted in the preface, *social life feeling* is defined as a sentiment about the social world—for example, the future of this country is bleak, the lot of the average man is getting worse, poor people could improve their lot if they tried, the world is too complicated for one to understand—or a feeling about the self in society— for example, I feel ignored by my peers, I seem to be marking time, I was happier as a child, I tend to get bored on the job. The term is used for both feeling-states.

The motivation behind our effort at scale construction lay in common practices in measuring social life feelings in American sociology during the period 1930–1970. The more relevant of these were the following:

1. The practice of using the same items in tests purporting to measure different constructs. For example, the alienation tests of the 1960s consist of many of the same items appearing in the morale tests of the 1930s.

2. The reverse practice of using different items in tests purporting to measure the same construct. A morale test of the 1960s may have little in common with morale tests of the 1930s; a later scale may be identical to earlier ones in name only (see Schuessler and Freshnock, 1978).

3. The practice of modifying a previously constructed test by either dropping or adding items or both, either for practical reasons (to get a shorter scale) or for theoretical reasons (to get rid of a priori meaningless items).

4. The practice of making up new scales when adequate ones already exist. A brand-new scale may represent an honest conviction that no previously constructed scale quite captures the essence of a particular concept or a judgment that no available scale is applicable to the special population under study (veterans, migrant workers).

All these specific tendencies add up to a general practice of tailoring the scale to meet what the investigator regards as the special requirements of a particular investigation, rather than using the same scale repeatedly in order to gain the advantages of replication. Only a handful of scales, if that, have been used with some regularity and by that criterion could be regarded as standard scales.

None of the above practices was planned; rather, all appear to be the crescive result of circumstances working for the appearance (and disappearance) of ad hoc scales and against the repeated use of the same scale. We here list a few of the most important of these circumstances:

1. *Item semantics.* A given social life feeling item ("America is sick") may mean different things to different people in the same population; it may change in meaning from time to time in the same population; it may differ in meaning from one population to another; it may have little or no meaning in any population. Items that have meaning for a political elite may have no meaning for the general public (Converse, 1964), and such items should probably not

be used in the general public at all (except to confirm the random nature of responses to them); their use should be limited to members of the political elite or to groups in which they are meaningful. Analogously, items that had meaning for measuring worker morale during the Great Depression of the 1930s may have little or no meaning for workers today because of changing idioms and jargons. The contingent meaning of an item in time and territory probably accounts for the tendency of researchers to paraphrase old items or to discard them for completely new ones or both.

2. *Concept differentiation.* The conceptualization of social life feelings has changed from time to time, and these changes have created a demand for new scales. The five forms of alienation, as brilliantly expounded by Seeman (1959), have been matched by as many separate scales. The different dimensions of external/internal control, as detailed by Gurin and others (1969), has led to a rescoring of the Rotter (1966) Internal External Control Scale. The now generally accepted difference between intrinsic and extrinsic job satisfaction has inspired a variety of scales for measuring different aspects of worker morale. In this way the differentiation of concepts has contributed to the creation of new scales and the modification of older ones.

3. *Scaling developments.* Attitude scaling started in the late 1920s with Thurstone's work on paired comparisons and equal-appearing intervals (Schuessler, 1971). Since then there has been a steady proliferation of scaling techniques, each claiming to be best suited for some particular purpose. A perhaps unintended consequence of these developments is that scales in use at the time have been abandoned not because of proven weaknesses but rather because of the perceived promise of the latest scaling techniques. Likert summation scales have been discarded in favor of Guttman simplex scales; Thurstone categorical judgment scales have been discarded for Stevens's ratio estimation scales. In this way, the development of scaling techniques has contributed to the turnover of social life feeling measures in sociology.

4. *Field and literature specialization.* The mushrooming of scales may be due in part to the separation of specialties both within and between the social sciences. The appearance of a new measure of normlessness in sociology may be due to lack of contact with related

work in the field of social psychiatry; similarly, the appearance of a
new measure of personal efficacy may be due to a lack of contact
with related work in the field of personality assessment. The tendency toward what might be called the provincialism of specialties
has thus contributed to the duplication of scaling efforts within and
between the social sciences. In sociology, essentially the same scale
has been invented several times, an instance of provincialism within
the same field.

Research Operations

In the face of many quite similar scales it was and is natural
to ask whether all the items appearing in them might reflect only a
few basic feelings and whether these few feelings might be reliably
represented by as many scales. In other words, we wondered whether
a few relatively independent scales might do the work of the many
overlapping scales. In answering that question, we carried out these
operations in roughly this sequence:

1. Canvassed sociological writings for terms denoting a sentiment about the social world (cynicism, pessimism) or an affect
   state presumably based on one's experiences in that world
   (demoralized, estranged).
2. Listed scales used in one way or another in sociology for
   measuring those concepts during the last fifty years or so.
3. Listed items appearing in those scales.
4. Purged this list of duplicate and seemingly extraneous items
   and classified the remaining items by broad topic.
5. Chose from this refined list a representative subset of 237 items
   for use in a sample survey questionnaire.
6. Administered this survey questionnaire to a national probability sample of 1,522 adults.
7. Scored responses for each of these 237 items and calculated all
   interitem correlations and their dimensionality.
8. Selected items to represent dimensions by the criterion that
   items within dimensions have a Tucker-Lewis reliability coefficient of approximately 0.90 and an alpha reliability of 0.80.

(Statistical formulas appear in Appendix E). The twelve social life feeling scales are the product of this selection process.

9. Investigated the efficacy of social life feeling scales in predicting social background (age, sex, marital status) and vice versa.
10. Investigated the dependence of social life feeling scores on acquiescing and responding desirably.

Related Work

Our study was not the first to explore the dimensionality of social life feeling items. The following studies were somewhat similar in method and purpose to ours.

Neal and Rettig (1963) investigated the relation between several measures of alienation and Srole's five-item anomia scale. From findings based on the responses of 603 residents of Columbus, Ohio, they concluded that normlessness and powerlessness, regarded as dimensions of alienation, are orthogonal to anomie, also viewed as an underlying dimension. Later, on reanalyzing the same data (1967) in line with suggestions made by Cartwright (1965), they modified their claim that these dimensions are strictly orthogonal and accepted the alternative that they are probably nonorthogonal.

Struening and Richardson (1965) gave sixty-eight items from previously constructed scales on alienation and anomie to 422 institutionalized subjects (prisoners, for example). The items composing Srole's anomie scale eventually became attached to their first-factor scale, which they took to be a measure of "alienation via rejection." This result suggests that anomie might be regarded as an aspect of alienation.

In a similar study, Dodder (1969) factor-analyzed the responses of 201 women (resident in five Kansas communities) to Dean's alienation scale of twenty-four items. He concluded that these items were measuring not normlessness, powerlessness, and social isolation, as claimed, but rather "unanticipated latent dimensions." He took the statistically strongest of these dimensions to be retreatist alienation.

Gurin and others (1969) examined the dimensionality of the twenty-three items making up Rotter's internal external control scale. From their findings based on a sample of 1,212 black college students, they concluded that Rotter's scale is multidimensional and, in particular, that items related to expectations for self (personal control) and items related to beliefs about others (ideology control) should be scored separately.

Cherline and Reeder (1975) investigated the dimensionality of the Bradburn-Caplovitz affect-balance scale. They administered this scale of 12 items in 1972 to 1,078 adults living in Los Angeles County and to a different sample of 1,008 adults in the same county in 1973. Their major conclusion, anticipated by Bradburn's less intricate statistical analysis, was that the affect-balance scale reflects two dimensions and that a separate score for each dimension should probably be calculated.

The studies cited above are similar to ours in their concern with the dimensionality of social life feeling tests and/or subsets of items appearing in those tests. They differ from ours in scope and method. Our sample of 1,522 cases was representative of the U.S. adult population at the time it was drawn. Such a broad sample permits various subgroups (age, education) to be reliably compared and weighted averages for all subgroups combined to be calculated. Such analysis is not possible with highly specialized samples (prison inmates, college students). The survey sample of 237 social life feeling items represents practically all items ever used for measuring social life feelings in U.S. sociology. Such a sample of materials permits the dimensionality of the largest possible pool of items to be estimated and scales for selected dimensions to be constructed. A highly specialized sample of items would not answer these objectives.

Scale Origins

Scales in use in sociology were not always constructed with the field of sociology uppermost in mind. In the process of collecting items it became evident that efforts to measure social life feelings were motivated as much by practical considerations as by theoretical ones and were often made in response to pressing social demands. Few scales appear to have been developed for the sole object of resolving a theoretical issue, and practically all answered to some social problem. As examples, we cite (1) the Depression of the 1930s,

(2) World War II, (3) automation in industry, and (4) old age and retirement.

1. Much of the work of social scientists in the 1930s bears the stamp of the Depression, and work on social discontent and social despair and on related social life feelings is no exception. The difficult circumstances in which many persons were placed during the Depression and the effect of these circumstances on morale were the subject of much discussion among social scientists (Stouffer and Lazarsfeld, 1937) and some systematic measurement.

For example, Rundquist and Sletto (1936) undertook to develop scales for measuring the effect of the Depression on morale, normlessness, disenchantment, and the like. They claimed that "the need for quantitative measures is particularly urgent at this time in view of the various educational and recreational programs that are being widely instituted to prevent the disintegration of personality that is presumed to accompany prolonged unemployment. Furthermore, quantitative measures devised now will permit the detection of future trends with respect to the traits measured" (p. 1). This work is also pertinent here in showing the tendency of items used in one period for one purpose to be used in a later period for another purpose.

2. The U.S. involvement in World War II had its impact on the work of social scientists in the 1940s, much as the Depression had shaped their work in the thirties. Their concern manifested itself at the start of the decade in a variety of articles on concepts and methods for understanding and predicting the reactions of civilians and soldiers to the uncertainties of war (*American Journal of Sociology*, 1941; *Annals of the American Academy of Political and Social Science*, 1941, 1942; Child, 1941). Much of this writing, while not challenging the usefulness of concepts such as morale and *esprit de corps*, nevertheless cited their elusive character, their multiple meanings, and their unsusceptibility to precise measurement.

Despite these recognized difficulties, social scientists did not back away from the chance to try their hand at measuring the attitudes of both civilians and soldiers toward the stressful circumstances in which they found themselves during the war. Stouffer and his associates (1949) undertook to measure the morale of American soldiers; the U.S. Strategic Bombing Survey (1947) sought to determine the effects of sustained bombing on the willingness of German civilians to give continued support to the war effort. In these latter studies, responses to questions on confidence and uncertainty were weighted and combined to yield an index of morale. Essentially the same questions have since been used in scales to measure concepts such as anomie and alienation.

3. That many American workers have the "blue-collar blues" is generally conceded. This phrase was coined apparently to draw attention to the dreary way in which many people spend their working days. This prolonged dreariness and its consequent demoralization are generally regarded as the price of technological and industrial progress. The idea is not new; it has been expressed repeatedly in both factual and fictional (for example, Samuel Butler's) writing during the last 150 years. Whatever its validity, it has stimulated a wide variety of efforts to measure alienation and related concepts. Sheppard and Herrick's (1972) study of worker dissatisfaction in the late 1960s and early 1970s supplies an example; *Work in America* (W.E. Upjohn Institute, 1973) contains numerous references and furnishes an entree to the literature.

4. For demographic reasons that are well known, the number of retired persons in America is steadily increasing. Judging from surveys, many older persons find retirement, and the social disengagement that comes in its wake, to be sad and lonely, as well as monotonous and dreary. Accordingly, we would anticipate that just as the dreariness of work has created a demand for information about its dimensions, so the demoralization of retirement has created a demand for information about its scope and causes. Countless studies, conducted largely during the last twenty-five years, reflect that demand; many of these (Cavan and others, 1949; Lowenthal, 1964) have focused on the morale of older persons and techniques for measuring it.

The conclusion to be drawn from the preceding cases is that efforts at measuring social life feelings have arisen largely in response to changing social circumstances and have been only incidentally related to theoretical issues in social science. When these issues were raised, they were often raised as an afterthought. Our content domain may thus be regarded as having been determined more by social problems than by social theory.

The diverse specialties to which scales may be traced is another indication that they were generally constructed for quite practical purposes. Although these specialties focus on different populations, or clienteles, they have in common the goal of a reliable quantitative index of some social life feeling. It is this common requirement that accounts for the representation of social psychiatry and opinion polling, to name two cases, in our domain. By way of elaboration:

1. In recent times, social psychiatrists have become increasingly concerned with the accuracy of their estimates of mental illness in the general population. This concern is behind various suggestions for getting more accuracy. The sample survey of the general population is one suggestion. These surveys, when carried out, usually cover both psychotic and sociopathic symptoms; and questions pertaining to sociopathic symptoms are often closely similar to questions pertaining to demoralization, despair, normlessness, and the like. Thus, the statement "It is all right to get around the law if you don't actually break it" may be taken in one questionnaire as an indicator of sociopathic tendency; in another, as an indicator of normlessness. What the social psychiatrist takes as a symptom of mental illness, the sociologist may take as a sign of normlessness. It is thus understandable that questions devised by social psychiatrists to measure mental illness have worked their way into questionnaires devised by sociologists to measure such concepts as anomie and social despair.

2. Efforts to gauge the public's confidence in the economy or its trust in the government, for example, account for the presence of opinion polling in our item pool. Polls on such matters are practically useful to politicians and businesspersons planning for the future; they are useful to sociologists for testing theoretical ideas. It is therefore not surprising that some scales to measure such topics as public confidence and trust consist almost entirely of items drawn from public opinion polls.

Opinion polling also enters the pool through its connection with social-indicator analysis and vice versa. To date, social indicators have been based largely on objective social statistics about income, education, housing, health, and so on. Lately, some attention has been given to monitoring the psychological well-being of the population. The work of Bradburn (1969) supplies one example, the work of Andrews and Withey (1976) another. Since questions on the perceived quality of life are closely similar to questions on morale, alienation, and the like, their presence in our set was an almost foregone conclusion.

In the end, the content domain gave the appearance of an orderly arrangement of 545 relatively simple statements. But its orderliness at the end should not be permitted to obscure either its arbitrary makeup or its origin in practical social endeavor. Its makeup is arbitrary because it rests on somewhat arbitrary decisions about what to include; it is practical in origin because it grows out of broad social problems, rather than basic theoretical issues.

In making up the content domain, we had to decide where to start the literature search; which scales to eliminate before screening items; which items to eliminate and which to keep. If we had started the search elsewhere, we would have come up with a different set of references; if we had eliminated fewer scales before screening items, we would have come up with a different pool of potential items; if we had discarded fewer items, we would have come up with a different set of items. We did try to create a domain that was reliable in the sense that anyone could construct it by following our steps.

Most if not all of the items in our domain had their origin in the efforts of social scientists to measure the subjective effects (morale, alienation, disenchantment) of some difficult life situation (unemployment, combat duty, retirement). In this view, the items are a response to a social problem rather than a response to a theoretical issue. The analysis of such an atheoretical domain is justified when the object is to investigate the dimensions present in scales that are, in some cases, nominally identical but substantively different and, in other cases, nominally different but substantively identical. A pool restricted to items expressive of a particular concept would be, from our standpoint, a form of question begging. Clustering among diverse but still closely related items could not be discerned if diversity were eliminated on a priori grounds at the start.

2

Using
Agree-Disagree Items
to Measure Feelings

This chapter presents twelve social life feeling scales (SLFSs). For each scale, we give the items composing it and what scores based on these items appear to be measuring; statistics for items and composites are also given. In describing and discussing scales first and the method of their construction second, we reverse the order of actual research operations. Our justification for this reversal is that the scales themselves will probably hold more interest for most readers than the technical details of their construction. (Scale construction is the subject of Chapter Three.)

The twelve scales collectively cover ninety-five items, fourteen of which appear in two scales each. All ninety-five items come from the same content domain, defined as items appearing in social life feeling questionnaires in use in American sociology during the last fifty years or so. We use the term *social life feelings* broadly to cover both sentiments about the social world (fatalism, pessimism, and so on) and affect states that come from living in that world (lonely, satisfied, depressed, and so on). The construction of the content domain is described in Appendix A.

The items were thus not original with us. We did change the wording of some in order that they might be answered more readily by "agree" or "disagree"; but in only a very few cases did we make up items from scratch. It would be fair to say that we did not invent new items, we merely rearranged old ones.

Of the ninety-five items appearing in all twelve SLFSs, eighty-two call for an answer of agree or disagree, and thirteen call for an answer of often, sometimes, seldom, or never. These latter thirteen items appear in three scales—Nos. 3, 11, and 12. All answers are scored 0 and 1, according to whether they express a relatively positive or relatively negative social life feeling. A positive feeling is by definition one that would normally be preferred to its opposite, which would then be defined as negative. By this criterion, the feeling of being satisfied with one's job is positive and feeling dissatisfied is negative.

Scores for responses to negative and positive items are as shown in Table 1. The keyed response (scored 1) is thus "agree" or "often" or "sometimes" for all negative statements; "disagree" or "seldom" or "never" for all positive statements. Reversing the key for all items would have no effect on score distributions and their correlations. Reversing the key in those cases in which the scale score runs counter to the scale concept (Nos. 4, 5, 6, and 10) would probably have practical advantages. Missing responses may be re-

Table 1. Item Scoring.

	Item	
Response	*Negative*	*Positive*
Agree	1	0
Disagree	0	1
Often	1	0
Sometimes	1	0
Seldom	0	1
Never	0	1

placed by 0, 1 responses with probabilities proportional to marginal frequencies. (See Appendix D for details.)

In its method of scoring, a SLFS is similar, at least superficially, to a true/false knowledge test—to get a score, one merely adds up the number of keyed answers. There is this obvious difference, however. The truth of a knowledge statement is based on fact, whereas the definition of a social life feeling statement as positive (or negative) is arbitrary in the sense that it rests on a social consensus, possibly unstable and subject to change. The truth of the statement "Columbus discovered America in 1492" rests on factual evidence that will hold indefinitely, whereas the definition of the statement "The lot of people is getting worse" as negative depends on a collective preference for things to get better rather than to get worse, a preference that conceivably could reverse itself in certain circumstances.

Scale interpretations were initially based on the items themselves, especially on those items with the highest item-total correlations. We inspected the items and then made our interpretation. Initial interpretations were later modified in the light of the relation of the SLFSs to differently constructed scales—author scales, topic scales, and subject-class scales. (These relations are considered in detail in Chapter Four.)

Here is an abbreviated example: After reviewing the items making up SLFS2, we concluded that scores based on them were probably an index of what we called "Social Trust." The term *trust* appeared in four of the eight items, including the statistically best item (item-total correlation = 0.57)—namely, "There are few people in this world you can trust, when you get right down to it." Later, after reviewing the correlations between SLFS2 and differently constructed scales (for example, Rosenberg's Faith in People Scale), we dropped the title "Social Trust" in favor of "Trustworthiness of People." This revised title seemed to convey more precisely the question answered by SLFS2 scores—namely, "Are people trustworthy?"

It is pertinent that scale interpretations came after item screening and selection—we first selected items and then undertook to interpret scores based on them. This reverses the usual procedure of defining a concept first and then finding a set of items expressive of that concept.

For each item in each scale we give the keyed response, the percentage keyed response (in our national sample), the item-total correlation, and factor loading. Keyed responses, after tallying, indicate whether a scale is key-balanced, key-uniform, or somewhere in between. (It is of interest that none of the twelve SLFSs was key-balanced.) The percentage keyed response indicates whether respondents were evenly divided between response categories or located mainly in one category or the other. (In constructing the survey questionnaire, we tried to eliminate items with highly skewed marginals. See Appendix B for details.)

The item-total correlation is the point-biserial correlation between item and total score with that item deleted. The factor loading, as here calculated, is simply the product-moment correlation between item and the first principal factor. Since factor loadings and item-total correlations are very nearly proportional, for all practical purposes we could get along with one series or the other.

For each SLFS, as part of the text, we give mean, median, and standard deviation. The mean score reflects the tendency toward negative responding in the sampled population; the mean score per item is the number of times in 100 that respondents accepted a negative scale item or rejected a positive one. The tendency toward score bunching and skew may be judged from the relation of mean to median, and both to standard deviation.

Also for each scale, in a single display (Table 2), we give number of items, mean interitem correlation, coefficient alpha, Tucker-Lewis reliability coefficient (TLRC), the first (largest) eigenvalue, correlation with first-factor score, and Guttman reproducibility. The mean interitem correlation gauges the tendency of respondents to give the keyed answer to both items in each of all pairs of items within scales. It may be regarded as a measure of concordant responding: the higher the mean correlation, the greater the degree of concordance in responding. Coefficient alpha is by definition the proportion of observed score variance attributable to true score variance (Appendix E); the Tucker-Lewis reliability coefficient is, in rough terms, the proportion of observed correlation between items (within scales) attributable to the first factor (Appendix E); the first eigenvalue, in a manner analogous to both alpha and TLRC, gives after division by the number of test items the proportion of aggregate variance attributable to the first factor.

Table 2. Twelve SLFSs: Number of Items (k), Mean Interitem Correlation ($\bar{r}_{ij}$), Alpha Reliability (α), Tucker-Lewis Reliability Coefficient (TLRC), First Eigenvalue (λ_1), Correlation with First-Factor Score (r_{xf}), Guttman Reproducibility (GR).

No.	Short Title	k	$\bar{r}_{ij}$	α	TLRC	λ_1	r_{xf}	GR
1	Self-determination	14	0.22	0.80	0.94	3.94	0.99	0.75
2	Distrust People	8	0.37	0.80	0.86	3.37	0.99	0.80
3	Feel Down	10	0.27	0.80	0.96	3.49	0.99	0.78
4	Job Satisfaction	9	0.25	0.75	0.92	3.06	0.99	0.80
5	Faith in Politics	10	0.20	0.71	0.92	2.83	0.99	0.73
6	Feel Up	11	0.21	0.75	0.94	3.19	0.99	0.77
7	People Cynicism	6	0.22	0.62	0.87	2.10	0.99	0.80
8	Political Cynicism	10	0.22	0.71	0.96	2.77	0.99	0.74
9	Future Outlook	12	0.23	0.78	0.96	3.60	0.99	0.74
10	Work Ethic	5	0.19	0.53	0.90	1.80	0.98	0.85
11	Demoralized	9	0.18	0.66	0.96	2.46	0.99	0.79
12	Career Concerns	6	0.24	0.65	0.91	2.33	0.99	0.84

The correlation between test scores (sums of keyed answers) and calculated factor scores (sums of weighted-by-least-squares keyed answers) indicates whether these latter quantities estimate more reliably the true (unobservable) factor scores than sums of keyed answers. When that correlation is 1.00, factor scores are no more reliable than unweighted scores and consequently carry no advantage; otherwise they would probably be preferred. With one exception (No. 10), all these correlations were larger than 0.995,, which means that, practically, crude scores will do as well as refined scores.

We give Guttman reproducibilities, mainly as a reminder that, for the same scale, reproducibility may be low and Tucker-Lewis reliability high (relatively).

Scale numbers correspond approximately to the order in which scales were constructed, first to last. Alternative methods of administering scales are described in Appendix B, on questionnaire construction and design.

SLFS1

Doubt About Self-Determination

The items of SLFS1 generally call into question the doctrine of self-determination, or individualism. Since all fourteen items are negative in direction, all are keyed "agree." Collectively these items portray the person as being shaped by social circumstances rather than as shaping them. They portray social circumstances as being indifferent to individual effort, rather than as reinforcing it. Persons scoring high see the social world as unresponsive to planning and work; persons scoring low express few such doubts, although they do not affirm their faith in the doctrine of self-determination. For that reason, we interpret this scale as a measure of doubt about self-determination. By the term *doubt,* we intend to indicate that scores correspond to feelings of doubt, high to low, rather than to feelings of doubt at one end and feelings of faith at the other.

Scores in the national sample ranged from 0 to 14. They had a mean of 5.69, a median of 5.28, and a standard deviation of 3.57. The mean score per item was 0.41, which means that respondents chose a negative (keyed) statement approximately four times in ten.

SLFS1 Doubt About Self-Determination.

Tape No.	Statement	Keyed Response	% Keyed Response	Item-Total Correlation	Factor Loading	Member of
3	There are few people in this world you can trust, when you get right down to it.	A	51	.45	.51	SLFS2
62	What happens in life is largely a matter of chance.	A	39	.47	.53	
64	If the odds are against you, it's impossible to come out on top.	A	34	.42	.47	
65	I have little influence over the things that happen to me.	A	33	.43	.49	SLFS11
66	I sometimes feel that I have little control over the direction my life is taking.	A	35	.44	.49	SLFS6
67	Nowadays a person has to live pretty much for today and let tomorrow take care of itself.	A	61	.46	.52	
81	I've had more than my share of troubles.	A	41	.43	.47	
82	For me one day is no different from another.	A	30	.41	.46	
91	The world is too complicated for me to understand.	A	48	.39	.44	SLFS11
113	I regret having missed so many chances in the past.	A	47	.33	.37	
126	It's unfair to bring children into the world with the way things look for the future.	A	35	.41	.46	
133	The future is too uncertain for a person to plan ahead.	A	49	.49	.55	SLFS9
136	I find it difficult to be optimistic about anything nowadays.	A	35	.43	.48	SLFS11
178	No right or wrong ways to make money, only easy and hard.	A	29	.32	.36	

SLFS2

Doubt About Trustworthiness of People

The eight items in SLFS2 pertain to the trustworthiness of people. Are people generally fair, forthright, and honest in their everyday life, or are they given to cheating, dissembling, and lying? Five of the items call into question the trustworthiness of others; three of the eight affirm their trustworthiness.

High scorers assent to negative statements and take exception to positive ones; low scorers reverse this pattern of responding. Low scorers feel that people are generally trustworthy, while high scorers have their doubts. It is therefore natural to interpret this scale as a measure of doubt about the trustworthiness of people.

Scores in the sample ranged from 0 to 8 around a mean of 3.97 and a median of 3.94; they had a standard deviation of 2.50. The mean per item was 0.50, which means that respondents chose either to accept a negative or to reject a positive statement one time in two.

SLFS2 Doubt About Trustworthiness of People.

Tape No.	Statement	Keyed Response	% Keyed Response	Item-Total Correlation	Factor Loading	Member of
1	It is hard to figure out who you can really trust these days.	A	63	.52	.58	
3	There are few people in this world you can trust, when you get right down to it.	A	51	.57	.64	SLFS1
13	Most people can be trusted.	D	35	.56	.63	
17	Strangers can generally be trusted.	D	65	.39	.44	
20	Most people are fair in their dealings with others.	D	26	.49	.55	
158	Most people don't really care what happens to the next fellow.	A	48	.54	.62	
159	Too many people in our society are just out for themselves and don't really care for anyone else.	A	62	.56	.64	SLFS7
175	Many people are friendly only because they want something from you.	A	47	.47	.53	SLFS7

SLFS3

Feeling Down

SLFS3 consists of ten items on social isolation and mental depression. These items afford respondents an opportunity to indicate whether they feel forgotten, depressed, lonely, isolated, detached, useless. High scorers reveal themselves as isolated and depressed; low scorers admit to no such portrayal of themselves. But low scorers would not necessarily agree to a view of themselves as happy and joyful; they only reject a picture of themselves as sad and lonely. For that reason, we call this scale the "feeling down scale." It arranges persons from high to low according to degree of feeling down.

Five items call for "agree" or "disagree," and five call for "often," "sometimes," "seldom," or "never" in answer to the question "How often did you feel this way during the past several weeks?" For these five items, the keyed response was either "often" or "sometimes."

Scores in the national sample ranged from 0 to 10. They had a mean of 3.14, a median of 2.56, and a standard deviation of 2.66. Respondents accepted statements of feeling down approximately three times in ten, as indicated by the mean item score of 0.30.

SLFS3 Feeling Down.

Tape No.	Statement	Keyed Response	% Keyed Response	Item-Total Correlation	Factor Loading
149	I feel that I'm not a part of things.	A	31	.50	.58
150	I feel somewhat apart even among friends.	A	28	.47	.54
151	I sometimes feel forgotten by friends.	A	24	.37	.55
155	At times I feel that I am a stranger to myself.	A	21	.44	.50
192	I just can't help feeling that my life is not very useful.	A	21	.45	.51
217	Very lonely or remote from other people.	O/S	22	.53	.61
221	Depressed or very unhappy.	O/S	33	.53	.60
223	Bored.	O/S	45	.43	.49
225	So restless you couldn't sit long in a chair.	O/S	41	.34	.37
227	Vaguely uneasy about something without knowing why.	O/S	47	.43	.47

O = Often
S = Sometimes

SLFS4

Job Satisfaction

SLFS4 consists of nine items on job satisfaction. Five are negative in direction; four are positive. High scorers put their work experience in an unfavorable light—they endorse negative statements and reject positive ones; low scorers reverse this pattern of responding. Scores thus arrange persons from high to low according to degree of job dissatisfaction as verbally expressed. Low scorers are presumably more satisfied, or less dissatisfied, with their jobs than high scorers.

Scores in the sample of 723 gainfully employed workers ranged from 0 to 9. They had a mean of 2.29, a median of 1.73, and a standard deviation of 2.21. The mean score per item was 0.30, indicating that respondents accepted expressions of job dissatisfaction three times in ten. It is of passing interest that the average amount of job dissatisfaction, as here indexed, is about equal to the average amount of feeling down, as gauged by SLFS3.

SLFS4 Job Satisfaction.

Tape No.	Statement	Keyed Response	% Keyed Response	Item-Total Correlation	Factor Loading
22	There is too little variety in my job.	A	18	.50	.59
23	I tend to get bored on the job.	A	24	.46	.56
24	There must be better places to work.	A	51	.41	.47
28	I would like more freedom on the job.	A	27	.36	.40
29	I have too small a share in deciding matters that affect my work.	A	25	.42	.49
31	My job means more to me than just money.	D	23	.45	.53
34	I am satisfied with the work I do.	D	16	.49	.58
35	My job gives me a chance to do what I do best.	D	25	.47	.56
39	People feel like they belong where I work.	D	19	.31	.35

SLFS5

Faith in Citizen Involvement

Feelings about the citizen and the government are indexed by SLFS5. Its main theme is the impact of the individual on the government and vice versa. Eight items are positive in direction, and two are negative.

All items, with one or two exceptions (depending on how they are construed), imply a discrepancy between the actual relation of government to individual in a political democracy and the ideal relation. For example, citizen involvement should make a difference, but it doesn't; people should have some say in the government, but they don't. For this reason we call this scale the "faith in citizen involvement scale." It might with equal justification be labeled the "faith in political democracy scale."

Low scorers view the government as accessible to the individual and responsive to his or her efforts and appeals; high scorers see the government as remote from the individual and unresponsive to his or her efforts and initiatives. SLFS5 may thus be taken as an index of faith in the democratic partnership between the government and the individual.

Scores in the national sample of 1,522 cases ranged from 0 to 10. They had a mean of 5.43, a median of 5.71, and a standard deviation of 2.52. The mean score per item was 0.54; that is, respondents gave the negative (keyed) answer 54 times in 100.

SLFS5 Faith in Citizen Involvement.

Tape No.	Statement	Keyed Response	% Keyed Response	Item-Total Correlation	Factor Loading	Member of
47	The public has little control over what politicians do in office.	A	6	.39	.46	
48	The average person can get nowhere by talking to public officials.	A	43	.36	.42	
53	The average citizen has considerable influence on politics.	D	69	.48	.61	
55	The average person has much to say about running local government.	D	55	.41	.51	
56	People like me have much to say about government.	D	57	.36	.43	
57	The average person has a great deal of influence on government decisions.	D	75	.50	.64	
58	The government is generally responsive to public opinion.	D	46	.28	.32	
59	I am usually interested in local elections.	D	30	.27	.30	
80	By taking an active part in political and social affairs the people can control world events.	D	44	.33	.39	
138	Taking everything into account, the world is getting better.	D	63	.29	.34	SLFS9

SLFS6

Feeling Up

This scale pertains to upbeat feelings. Upbeat feelings take their meaning from downbeat feelings, and vice versa. Upbeat feelings are feelings that people would rather have if given a choice, and downbeat feelings are feelings that people would rather not have if given a choice. Most people would rather be happy than sad, satisfied than dissatisfied, and so on.

Eight of the eleven items in this scale are positive in direction. These eight present a picture of enjoyment, happiness, contentment, optimism, purpose. Three items are negative and present the opposite view. High scorers reject a picture of their feelings as upbeat; low scorers accept that picture. (If the key were reversed, high scores would correspond to acceptance of self-feelings as upbeat and low scores to rejection of that view. Such scoring, which would leave the score distribution unchanged, would be more consistent with the title "feeling up.")

Scores ranged from 0 to 11 in the national sample. They had a mean of 3.03, a median of 2.41, and a standard deviation of 2.57. The mean score per item was 0.27; in other words, respondents chose the negative (keyed) answer 27 times in 100. This figure and the corresponding figure of 0.30 for SLFS3 suggest that respondents are generally more willing to endorse a negative statement than to reject a positive one.

SLFS6 Feeling Up.

Tape No.	Statement	Keyed Response	% Keyed Response	Item-Total Correlation	Factor Loading	Member of
66	I sometimes feel I have little control over the direction my life is taking	A	35	.38	.44	SLFS1
79	When I make plans, I am almost certain that I can make them work.	D	20	.29	.34	
84	I was happier as a child than I am now.	A	27	.35	.41	
85	I couldn't be much happier.	D	41	.40	.47	
88	I get a lot of fun out of life.	D	16	.51	.60	
119	I am satisfied with the way things are working out for me.	D	22	.47	.55	
137	The future looks very bright to me.	D	40	.42	.49	SLFS9
144	Things get better for me as I get older.	D	31	.49	.57	
161	I have a great deal in common with most people.	D	19	.28	.32	
191	I seem to be marking time these days.	A	31	.41	.47	SLFS11
199	There is much purpose to what I am doing at present.	D	20	.37	.43	

SLFS7

People Cynicism

A view of people as self-serving, insincere, and aimless is conveyed by the six items of SLFS7. Two items (10, 159) show people as self-centered, or selfish; two answer the question whether people know what to do with their lives (107, 189). No. 175 portrays people as insincere, and No. 160 pictures people as lonely and socially unattached. Collectively, the six items put people in a cynical light—as having no definite goals, as being motivated by self-interest without regard for the well-being of others. For that reason we call this the "people cynicism scale." High scorers accept a cynical view of people; low scorers reject that view (but would not necessarily subscribe to an idealistic view of people as honest, sincere, and socially conscious). This scale thus arrays respondents from low to high according to degree of cynicism about people generally.

Scores in the national sample ranged from 0 to 6 around a mean of 4.00. The mean score per item was 0.67. The median score was 4.25; the standard deviation was 1.58.

SLFS7 People Cynicism.

Tape No.	Statement	Keyed Response	% Keyed Response	Item-Total Correlation	Factor Loading	Member of
10	In a society where almost everyone is out for himself, people soon come to distrust each other.	A	84	.33	.44	
107	Most people know what to do with their lives.	D	49	.27	.34	
159	Too many people in our society are just out for themselves and don't really care for anyone else.	A	62	.44	.60	SLFS2
160	Many people in our society are lonely and unrelated to their fellow human beings.	A	79	.32	.42	
175	Many people are friendly only because they want something from you.	A	47	.37	.50	SLFS2
189	Many people don't know what to do with their lives.	A	79	.39	.49	

SLFS8

Disillusionment with Government

SLFS8 is similar in content to SLFS5; seven of its nine items pertain to the relation of government to the individual. They differ in the direction of their items. The items in SLFS5 are mainly positive—eight of ten; the items of SLFS8 are mainly negative—seven of nine.

High scorers on SLFS5 repudiate the idealistic view of government as accessible and responsive to the citizen, while high scorers on SLFS8 accept the cynical view of government as indifferent to the citizen, perhaps scornful of him or her. Low scorers on SLFS5 endorse the idealistic view; low scorers on SLFS8 reject the cynical view. However, persons scoring low on SLFS5 do not necessarily score low on SLFS8. Substantively, this means that a person may reject a cynical view of government and still not accept an idealistic one. Or one may reject an idealistic position and still not adopt a cynical stance. In this respect, the relation of SLFS8 and SLFS5 is similar to the relation of SLFS3 and SLFS6. Respondents not portraying themselves as feeling up do not necessarily portray themselves as feeling down. In an analogous manner, persons repudiating an idealistic picture of government do not always adopt a cynical attitude.

Since SLFS8 reflects a degree of disillusionment with some articles of the democratic creed, we call it simply "disillusionment with government." Scores arrange persons from high to low according to the degree of that disillusionment.

Scores in the national sample had a mean of 4.92, a median of 5.12, and a standard deviation of 2.40; they ranged from 0 to 9. The mean score per item was 0.62.

SLFS8 Disillusionment with Government.

Tape No.	Statement	Keyed Response	% Keyed Response	Item-Total Correlation	Factor Loading	Member of
16	Most supermarkets are honestly run.	D	31	.29	.33	
41	We are slowly losing our freedom to the government.	A	65	.41	.49	SLFS9
42	Most politicians are more interested in themselves than in the public.	A	70	.48	.58	
43	I have little confidence in the government today.	A	58	.42	.51	SLFS9
46	The government is run by a few people in power.	A	67	.38	.46	
50	There's little use writing to public officials because they often aren't really interested in the problems of the average man.	A	48	.41	.49	
60	Public officials work for the people and not just for themselves.	D	51	.32	.39	
207	Our local government costs the taxpayer more than it is worth.	A	58	.37	.45	
208	In my opinion, this country is sick.	A	44	.42	.51	SLFS9

SLFS9

Future Outlook

With three exceptions, the twelve items in SLFS9 pertain to current and anticipated trends in the quality of social life. Six items suggest a deterioration in that quality, and three (Nos. 105, 137, 138) indicate that matters are improving or at least not getting worse. Three items (Nos. 43, 133, 208) appear to be only remotely related to one's outlook on the future.

A high score corresponds to a gloomy or pessimistic outlook; a low score registers a relatively favorable outlook. Since extreme scores require that positive and negative items be answered differently, we call this scale the "future outlook scale" rather than simply "pessimism" or "optimism." We interpret it as a measure of one's feeling about the future.

Scores ranged from 0 to 12 around a mean of 6.97 and a somewhat higher median of 7.40. The standard deviation was 3.13; the mean score per item was 0.58.

SLFS9 Future Outlook.

Tape No.	Statement	Keyed Response	% Keyed Response	Item-Total Correlation	Factor Loading	Member of
41	We are slowly losing our freedom to the government	A	65	.42	.48	SLFS8
43	I have little confidence in the government today.	A	58	.46	.52	SLFS8
98	Many things our parents stood for are going down the drain.	A	77	.37	.41	
105	Although things keep changing all the time, one still knows what to expect from one day to another.	D	55	.30	.35	
125	The lot of the average man is getting worse, not better.	A	53	.47	.54	
128	The future looks very bleak.	A	46	.55	.63	
172	More people will be out of work in the next few years.	A	75	.33	.38	
133	Friends are easy to find.	D	49	.43	.49	
134	The future of this country is very uncertain.	A	72	.51	.58	
137	The future looks very bright to me.	D	40	.40	.45	SLFS6
138	Taking everything into account, the world is getting better.	D	63	.45	.51	SLFS5
208	In my opinion, this country is sick.	A	44	.38	.43	SLFS8

SLFS10

Economic Self-Determination

This scale pertains to the question whether people could raise their economic status if they tried. Three of its five items (Nos. 73, 75, 78) give an affirmative answer to that question; one (No. 211) carries a negative answer; and the remaining item (No. 77) is only obliquely related to that issue.

High scorers reject the idea that people have only themselves to blame for their poor economic showing; they appear to put the blame on social circumstances. Low scorers reverse this pattern and appear to blame the individual rather than society. Since scores reflect the feeling that one's economic status is self-determined, we call this scale by that name.

Scores ranged from 0 to 5; they had a mean of 1.67, a median of 1.47, and a standard deviation of 1.26. The mean score per item was 0.33.

SLFS10 Economic Self-Determination.

Tape No.	Statement	Keyed Response	% Keyed Response	Item-Total Correlation	Factor Loading
73	Individuals are poor because of the lack of effort on their part.	D	53	.33	.51
75	Anyone can raise his standard of living if he is willing to work at it.	D	11	.32	.45
77	Most people have a good deal of freedom in deciding how to live.	D	24	.26	.37
78	Poor people could improve their lot if they tried.	D	20	.40	.62
211	Our country has too many poor people who can do little to raise their standard of living.	A	65	.20	.26

SLFS11

Feeling Demoralized

This scale reflects a feeling of demoralization, and we call it by that name. It gives respondents an opportunity to say whether they are marking time, find it difficult to be optimistic about anything, regard the world as too complicated to understand; also, whether they are pleased about having accomplished something and whether they consider themselves to be in good physical condition.

High scorers present a picture of self as useless, helpless, aimless; low scorers admit to no such picture of self. It would thus appear that this scale comes closest to the concept of morale and its connotations of demoralization and despair. Persons of low morale have little hope and have presumably stopped trying; persons of high morale have high hopes and persevere.

It is of passing interest that most of the items in this scale have appeared in questionnaires for gauging the morale of older people. This scale may thus find its principal utility in studies of the aged.

Scores in the national sample ranged from 0 to 9. They had a mean of 2.40, a median of 2.04, and a standard deviation of 1.99. The mean score per item was 0.27; that is to say, respondents gave the keyed (negative) answer 27 times in 100.

SLFS11 Feeling Demoralized.

Tape No.	Statement	Keyed Response	% Keyed Response	Item-Total Correlation	Factor Loading	Member of
65	I have little influence over the things that happen to me.	A	33	.38	.47	SLFS1
87	I consider myself to be in good physical condition.	D	18	.27	.33	
91	The world is too complicated for me to understand.	A	48	.32	.38	SLFS1
117	Compared to others, my life is not too good.	A	11	.34	.42	
136	I find it difficult to be optimistic about anything nowadays.	A	36	.36	.44	SLFS1
191	I seem to be marking time these days.	A	31	.37	.47	SLFS6
194	I can't do much for other people.	A	23	.39	.49	
216	On top of the world.	SL/N	33	.37	.47	
222	Pleased about having accomplished something.	SL/N	09	.28	.35	

SL = Seldom
N = Never

SLFS12

Career Concerns

Amount of time spent thinking about the demands and expectations of social living is indexed by SLFS12. It consists of six items from Bradburn and Caplovitz' original list of ten items on worries. Items were prefaced by the question "How often was each of these things on your mind in the last few weeks?" Respondents were given a choice of often, sometimes, seldom, or never. For purposes of dichotomous scoring, adjacent answers were combined and 1 assigned to often and sometimes and 0 to seldom and never.

Persons scoring high reported spending more time thinking about their practical problems than persons scoring low. Scores thus permit respondents to be arrayed from low to high according to their tendency to dwell mentally on such matters as money, marriage, and work. For that reason we call SLFS12 scores "career concerns scores" and the test itself the "career concerns scale."

We note in passing that SLFS12 was constructed independently of the other 11 SLFSs; we explain its separate construction in the next chapter.

Scores ranged from 0 to 6 with a mean of 4.27, a median of 4.58, and a standard deviation of 1.57. Respondents gave the keyed response 71 times in 100; in other words, the mean score per item was 0.71.

SLFS12 Career Concerns.

Tape No.	Statement[a]	Keyed Response	% Keyed Response	Item-Total Correlation	Factor Loading
E 1	Money	O/S	87	.26	.34
E 3	Work	O/S	78	.43	.54
E 4	Marriage	O/S	49	.36	.45
E 5	Getting ahead	O/S	70	.48	.64
E 6	Bringing up children	O/S	61	.37	.45
E 10	Future	O/S	82	.42	.54

[a]Question: "How often was each of these things on your mind in the last few weeks?"

Summary and Comment

Table 2 is a comparison of the twelve SLFSs in respect to their internal characteristics. It serves to bring out their similarities and differences.

The longest scale (No. 1) had fourteen items; the shortest (No. 10) had five. This comparison raises the question whether longer scales are better than shorter scales. Longer scales take more time to give and by that criterion are practically less useful; however, longer scales are more reliable than shorter scales, other things equal, and by that criterion are more useful. But when other things are not equal, no such easy generalization is possible. For example, SLFS1 is longer ($k = 14$) than SLFS2 ($k = 8$) but no more reliable, whereas SLFS4 is more reliable (0.75) than SLFS11 (0.66) but no longer ($k = 9$).

Alpha reliabilities ranged from 0.53 (No. 10) to 0.80 (Nos. 1 and 2). The question whether more reliable scales are better than less reliable scales is, in a sense, rhetorical. It is almost true by definition that, as between two measures, the more reliable one is better. But this rule stated out of context is misleading. Although a reliability of 0.80 is better than a reliability of 0.70, it still may not be good enough. A physician would probably discard a thermometer whose reliability was less than, say, 0.995. Furthermore, if sociological relevance is a criterion, one may either have to make do with a relatively unreliable scale or use no scale at all. If readings on morale are required, one will have to use the best available measure, even though that measure may not be very good (reliable).

Tucker-Lewis reliability coefficients (percentage reduction in baseline χ^2) ran from a low of 0.86 to a high of 0.96. As with alpha reliabilities, one might suppose that scales with higher Tucker-Lewis reliabilities are superior to scales with lower coefficients. They are by that criterion alone. But a scale rating high by that standard may rate low on some other standard. For example, SLFS11 has one of the highest Tucker-Lewis coefficients but a relatively low alpha reliability (0.66). For that reason, it would be impracticable to judge a scale by Tucker-Lewis reliability alone. Furthermore, as intimated above, unless substantive relevance is taken into account, it would be possible to adopt an excellent statistical scale that was only remotely related to the substantive issue or hypothesis.

These issues are discussed in Chapter Seven.

3

Selecting Statements and Constructing the Scales

In constructing scales our starting point was the replies of 1,522 randomly selected U.S. adults to 237 social life feeling items. These 237 items were chosen from a list of 545 items that in turn came from a screening of over 950 items. The method of selecting items is described in Appendix B; the survey interview is described in Appendix C.

Responses were scored 0 or 1 according to whether they reflected a positive or negative feeling. Missing responses were scored with probabilities proportional to marginal frequencies for responses not missing (detail in Appendix D).

After scoring all items, we correlated each with every other by the product-moment formula. The resulting coefficients were then factor-analyzed to determine the dimensionality of the common-factor space. We took this number to be seventeen. Finally we sought to represent each of these seventeen factors by a score based on items having only that factor in common. This last step brought us to the twelve SLFSs; these twelve scales correspond to what proved to be the most scalable factors.

Scale Criteria

In selecting items to represent factors, we did not require that they literally have only one factor in common; we required only that the Tucker-Lewis reliability coefficient (Appendix E) for that factor be 0.90 or higher and that that factor alone have an eigenvalue larger than 1.00. In other words, we required that items conform only approximately to the one-factor (Spearman's two-factor) model,

$$Y_{ij} = a_i F + b_i U_i$$

where Y_{ij} = response of jth person to ith item, a_i = weight of common factor F in ith item, b_i = weight of unique factor U_i in ith item.

We placed no restriction on the magnitudes of the disturbance terms (the U_i) individually; however, we did restrict their average magnitude within scales. In placing no restrictions on the magnitudes of the U_i, one runs the risk of getting items that are unreliable predictors of one another (weakly correlated) while still being homogeneous in the sense of having only one factor in common (to the aforesaid approximation). To forestall that eventuality, we required that items within scales have a mean correlation in the neighborhood of 0.25. The sense of this requirement was that composite scores based on fifteen or so items have an alpha reliability no smaller than 0.80. As it turned out, only two of the twelve scales came up to this standard. In constructing scales, we discovered what we might have surmised in advance—namely, that in dropping items to raise the Tucker-Lewis reliability coefficient, we usually lost a little in alpha reliability; and, the reverse, when we added items to improve alpha reliability, we generally gave up a little in the way of Tucker-Lewis reliability.

From the above account, it is clear that criteria for scales represent more the upper limit of what is possible than an absolute ideal. Ideally, scale items would have only one factor in common and nothing else; in that case the Tucker-Lewis reliability coefficient would be very nearly equal to 1.00. Similarly, in the ideal case, scale scores would be completely free of measurement error, and the alpha reliability coefficient would be very nearly 1.00.

But to insist on these standards would be to do without scales, since they are practically out of reach. It is therefore necessary to adapt standards to the limitations of the observed data, possibly inherent. The requirement that the Tucker-Lewis reliability coefficient be at least 0.90 and that alpha reliability be at least 0.80 is one such adaptation. In another view, it is a reminder that combinations of social life feeling items usually have more than one common factor and that scores based on such combinations are limited in their reliability.

Choice of Coefficient

Since all responses were scored 0 or 1, all interitem correlations were based on the fourfold table. Furthermore, since we had defined a scale in terms of product-moment correlations, we were limited, at least in theory, to a product-moment formula. Consequently, for all practical purposes, we had to choose between the measure of product-moment correlation in the fourfold table—the phi coefficient (formula in Appendix E)—and an approximation of the normal bivariate product-moment correlation that could have given rise to the fourfold table of observed cell frequencies. This is the tetrachoric correlation coefficient (Appendix E).

As between these two measures, we chose the phi coefficient. In this choice, we were influenced by the following considerations: (1) the phi coefficient is an exact description of product-moment correlation in the 2×2 table; (2) it is free of assumptions about underlying variables; (3) upon factoring, it gives coefficients that may be regarded as point biserial correlations (see Appendix E); and (4) a phi matrix, because it is Gramian (symmetric and semipositive definite), lends itself to factor analysis. A disadvantage of phi is that its range is limited unless items (variables) are identical in their marginals. However, dividing phi by its maximum possible value for a coefficient that ranges from -1 to $+1$ seems to carry no advantages in scale construction (Carroll, 1961).

Phi coefficients and tetrachoric coefficients for items all (237) at a time could differ in their factor solutions (Arminger, 1979) and correspondingly in their assignment of items to scales. However, we made no such comparison. We did analyze interitem tetrachoric correlations within each of the 12 SLFSs. Our general finding was that these tetrachoric coefficients were no less (nor more) consistent with the one-factor model (to the required approximation) than were the phi coefficients. This is not surprising, since the interitem tetrachorics within scales were an almost perfect linear function of their corresponding phi coefficients.

Distribution of Phi

The phi coefficients were generally small and positive, as indicated by the class frequencies in Table 3. The generally positive correlation reflects the tendency of respondents to express themselves consistently in either a positive or a negative direction; the generally low correlation (mean = 0.073) indicates that this tendency toward consistent responding was weak or that responding inconsistently was not at all infrequent.

Since the phi coefficients were small (70 percent between −0.10 and +0.10), it was a foregone conclusion that the communalities of items within scales would be small and that items within scales would therefore be only weakly correlated with their underlying factor. For the same reason, it was a foregone conclusion that alpha reliability would be low (being a function of average interitem correlation). The generally weak correlation left open the question of homogeneity of items within scales, or the Tucker-Lewis reliabil-

Table 3. Class Frequencies of Phi Coefficients.

Lower Limit	Frequency (Percent)
−0.99	7.7
−0.02	14.4
0.02	23.8
0.06	22.6
0.10	14.4
0.14	8.4
0.18	8.7
	100.0 (N = 25,651)

ity coefficient, since it is possible for items within scales to be only weakly correlated and still be high in their homogeneity. However, the main message of the phi coefficients was that even perfectly homogeneous scales of ten and fifteen items (Tucker-Lewis reliability coefficient = 1.00) would not be highly reliable.

Selecting Items for Scales

Our substantive assumption was that the 237 items expressed a relatively small number of primary feelings and that each of these could be represented by a scale. The corresponding statistical assumption was that the interitem correlations would show relatively few factors and that each could be reliably measured by relatively few items. We visualized a solution with no more large loadings (as defined) than items, and large loadings evenly divided among factors.

To check this possibility, we carried out a factor analysis of 237 items all at a time. In analyzing items all at a time, we were forced to drop a few items, since it was mechanically possible to handle only 230 items all at a time. From preliminary runs we had concluded that the ten items on fears and worries were only marginally related to the rest of the items; consequently, we decided to eliminate those ten items. This left us with a total of 227 items on which to run the analysis.

We took out the first sixteen principal factors and rotated to simple structure. Analyzing sixteen rather than, say, fifteen or seventeen factors was somewhat arbitrary. The first sixteen all had roots larger than 1.00 and by that criterion were significant. Differences between successive roots after the sixteenth were fairly constant; by that criterion, factors beyond the sixteenth were not significant.

The result of this factoring corresponded not at all to the simple pattern we had envisaged; most factors loaded in two or more items, and many items had loadings on two or more factors. Furthermore, large loadings were concentrated in a few factors; for example, the first factor alone had more loadings in excess of 0.30 than the last eight factors combined.

Our conclusion at this point was that we would have to screen items within factors in order to get combinations that met scale criteria. It should be mentioned that, in screening items, we relied solely on our statistical results: we did not drop items that seemed on the surface trivial or bizarre, nor did we keep items that had great substantive appeal. Our screening was purely mechanical.

As a first step, we dropped from each factor all items whose loadings on that factor were smaller than 0.20, or items that we supposed has no chance of being chosen to represent that factor. This screening gave us sixteen sets, ranging in size from two to eighty-three items. Second, from each of these once-reduced sets, we dropped items whose loadings were not among the twenty largest on that factor. After that cut, we had sixteen sets ranging in size from two to twenty. The sense of this reduction was that no social life feeling scale have more than twenty items (or that no scale take more than a few minutes to administer).

Third, we arbitrarily dropped five factors that we judged not to be amenable to reliable scaling because they respectively had so few loadings larger than 0.20. In effect, although not by rule, we dropped all sets with fewer than ten loadings larger than 0.20. This left us with eleven sets of items, ranging in size from ten to twenty.

As our fourth and final step, we screened items within sets, dropping them one at a time until the remaining items had a Tucker-Lewis reliability coefficient in the close vicinity of 0.90 and no more than one eigenvalue larger than 1.00.

In screening items within sets, our procedure was to drop on each trial whichever item had the largest average residual correlation after adjusting for the effect of the first principal factor. On the first trial, we dropped whichever item in the starting set had the largest average residual correlation; on the second trial, we dropped whichever item in the once-reduced set had the largest residual correlation. We continued sequentially in this manner until the $k = n - m$ items (n = starting number, m = number of dropped items) were a scale by our approximation rule.

Applying this procedure to all eleven sets gave us eleven social life feeling scales, later numbered 1 through 11. Each of these scales corresponds to a factor in the 227×227 correlation matrix, and each was arrived at by either factor-analyzing the twenty items with the largest loadings on that factor or by analyzing all items with loadings larger than 0.20 on that factor (when fewer than twenty items had loadings larger than 0.20). Together these eleven scales include eighty-nine different items, fourteen of which appear in more than one scale (see Chapter Two for detail).

At this juncture, we returned to the ten items on worries that had been excluded from the factor analysis for mechanical reasons. We had reason to believe that these ten items would have yielded another factor if they had been factored together with all the rest, since they were relatively strong in their correlations with one another and relatively weak in their correlations with all other items. In fact, this was our main justification for treating them separately in the first place and possibly representing them by a scale.

A factoring of these ten items showed two factors and correspondingly two fairly distinct clusters. The larger cluster was made up of six items on getting ahead socially, or making it; the smaller cluster had the four items on sickness, health, and death. SLFS12 is the cluster of six items on what we later called career concerns. Adding these six items to the eighty-nine appearing in Nos. 1–11 gave us a total of ninety-five items for all twelve social life feeling scales.

Interscale Correlations

In screening items, we did not require that items between scales literally have nothing in common; we required only that 90 percent of the correlation of items within scales be attributable to one factor and that that factor alone have an eigenvalue larger than 1.00. Items between scales would be perfectly uncorrelated if they had absolutely nothing in common. But the condition was not set; hence, it was an almost foregone conclusion that items from different scales would be correlated to some degree, as would, therefore, the scales themselves, since an interscale correlation is a function of the interitem correlations across scales.

From a statistical point of view, the interscale correlations thus do no more than describe the degree of correlation between items across scales. They may approximate the degree of correlation between social life feelings, and on the assumption that they do, an analysis of their pattern would indicate whether feelings tend to cluster and possibly suggest why. With these ideas in mind, we undertook to cluster the twelve scales on the basis of their varimax loadings, taking two or more scales as a cluster if they had the same simple pattern of loadings.

But before doing the factor analysis, we had to decide which correlations to analyze. The twelve scales could be paired in sixty-six ways, and nine of these pairs had one or more common items. The corresponding correlations (nine) could be calculated with common items removed from both scales, from one but not the other, or from neither. Since the smallest and largest correlations, corresponding to items deleted from both scales or neither, were most likely to produce contradictory results, we decided to limit the analysis to those extremes. As it turned out, the differences between these nine correlations did not produce a difference in the clustering of the twelve scales.

Common Items Present. The sixty-six correlations above the diagonal of Table 4 included nine with one or more common items. On factoring these sixty-six correlations, we obtained three significant factors, or three possible clusters. Varimax loadings on these three factors are given in Table 5(a). Dropping scales that had no simple pattern (one large loading, two small)—namely, Nos. 1, 10, and 11, left us with nine scales for clustering. Of these nine, Nos. 2, 5, 7, 8, and 9 had the same simple pattern and were a cluster by that criterion; Nos. 3, 4, and 6 were a cluster by the same criterion. Although No. 12 had a simple pattern, it could not by itself be considered a cluster, since a cluster requires at least two members. Disregarding No. 12 left us with two clusters of five and three scales.

A positive or negative feeling about society in general could account for the correlations between the scales in Cluster I: cynicism about people is measured by Nos. 2 and 7; cynicism about government and politicians is measured by Nos. 5 and 8; pessimism about trends in the quality of social life is measured by No. 9. Similarly, a positive or negative feeling about the self in general could account for the correlations between the scales in Cluster II: feeling down is measured by No. 3; feeling up is measured by No. 6; and feeling satisfied on the job is measured by No. 4. Each of these three scales pertains to a particular self-feeling. By the same logic, a general social life feeling, cutting across feelings about both society and self,

Table 4. Correlations Between Twelve Social Life Feeling Scales.

	1	2	3	4	5	6	7	8	9	10	11	12
1		53	41	27	28	52	31	47	59	12	74	-13
2	44		27	22	31	30	67	47	54	14	39	01
3				30	20	50	20	25	32	19	40	12
4					23	34	14	21	22	12	28	03
5						27	23	47	49	20	22	-02
6	43						23	28	46	27	60	-04
7		34						36	41	15	24	04
8									68	17	36	-07
9	52				39	36		41		20	44	-09
10											11	05
11	51					51						21
12												

Note: Correlations with common items deleted below diagonal.

could account for the relatively high correlation between Scale 1 and the other eleven scales (excepting No. 10), and also the relatively high loadings of all three factors in this scale, on the assumption that No. 1 is an index of that feeling.

Common Items Absent. The adjusted correlations (no common items present) are given below the diagonal in Table 4. On substituting these adjusted correlations for their counterparts above the line and factoring all sixty-six correlations, we obtained the varimax loadings shown in Table 5(b). As with the unadjusted results, the same three scales had no simple pattern; the same five scales had a relatively high loading on Factor 1; the same three had a relatively high loading on Factor 2; No. 12 again had a relatively high loading on Factor 3.

Since clusters based on adjusted correlations did not differ from those based on the unadjusted correlations, they do not differ in their implications. They imply a general feeling about self, a general feeling about society, and a general feeling about both self and society.

Factoring of Ninety-Five SLFS Items

The correlations between scales raised the further question whether the twelve scales could be recovered more or less intact from

Table 5. Factor Loadings (Varimax) on Twelve SLFSs.

Scale Number	Title	(a) Common Items Present Factor			(b) Common Items Deleted Factor		
		I	II	III	I	II	III
1	Doubt About Self-Determination	.45	.48	.52	.50	.45	.27
2	Doubt About Trustworthiness of People	.72	.21	.10	.62	.25	.07
3	Feeling Down	.18	.65	-.03	.20	.68	-.11
4	Job Satisfaction	.18	.41	.00	.20	.39	-.03
5	Faith in Citizen Involvement	.48	.23	.00	.52	.18	-.04
6	Feeling Up	.21	.73	.19	.23	.71	.08
7	People Cynicism	.61	.13	-.02	.49	.16	-.03
8	Disillusionment with Government	.68	.19	.16	.68	.18	.09
9	Future Outlook	.72	.31	.21	.65	.30	.16
10	Economic Self-Determination	.18	.27	-.12	.20	.23	-.13
11	Feeling Demoralized	.23	.57	.67	.32	.56	.45
12	Career Concerns	-.01	.09	-.38	-.02	.05	-.53

a separate factoring of the ninety-five items appearing in them. To check this possibility, we factor-analyzed the correlations between these ninety-five items all at a time and calculated the varimax loadings on the first twelve factors. We then listed the 109 (109 = number of times ninety-five items appeared in all twelve scales) largest loadings by factor and the item corresponding to each of these loadings. Of the ninety-five items, seventy-two were represented by one loading each, seventeen by two loadings each, and one item by three loadings. Five items (Nos. 59, 161, 208, 216, 222) appeared on no list.

Next we looked for and located the SLFS to which each list most nearly corresponded, and counted the items common to list and scale. Table 6 shows the detail.

Table 6. Distribution of Scale Items by Factoring.

List No.	1	2	3	4	5	6	7	8	9	10	11	12
Number of Items on List	23	8	11	9	7	11	7	9	12	5	1	6
Closest SLFS	1	2	3	4	5	6	7	8	9	10	4	12
Number of Items in SLFS	14	8	10	9	10	11	6	9	12	5	9	6
Number of Common Items	14	8	10	9	7	9	6	8	11	5	1	6

Of the twelve lists, four (Nos. 2, 4, 10, and 12) were perfectly matched with a SLFS; two (Nos. 3 and 7) differed in the addition of a single item; two (Nos. 8 and 9) differed in the replacement of a single item; one (No. 6) differed in the replacement of two items; and one (No. 5) differed in the deletion of three items. Ten of the twelve SLFSs were thus recovered more or less intact by the factoring of the ninety-five items appearing in all twelve scales.

SLFS1 and SLFS11 were the exceptions. SLFS1 was the best match for the twenty-three items on List 1; all fourteen of its items appeared on that list. The lone item (No. 28) on List 11 appeared in SLFS4. SLFS11 was thus lost in the process of factoring and listing all ninety-five items; SLFS1 was recovered but with a surplus of nine items.

An implication is that SLFS11 be dropped from the battery of twelve scales and that SLFS1 be lengthened. A case could be made for dropping SLFS11—its contents were largely (six of nine items) taken over by Factor (List) 1. However, it would be impossible to lengthen SLFS1 by more than a few items and still approximate scale criteria.

Scale Construction in Perspective

From the foregoing account, and the detail on which it rests, it is clear that the twelve SLFSs are contingent on judgments made concerning their construction. At the very beginning, we had to define the content domain in somewhat abstract terms; we defined it as items appearing in tests in use in sociology for measuring such concepts as morale and despair, cynicism and pessimism. Second, we had to compile a list of those tests and/or the items appearing in them. Third, from the list of items, once compiled, we had to choose a subset of items for inclusion in the survey questionnaire. Since interviewing time was limited, we could use only a fraction of the items; we had to decide on which ones. Fourth, we had to decide on the number and content of the answer categories—for example, whether to present "agree" and "disagree" or "strongly agree," "agree," "disagree," and "strongly disagree"; whether to offer "don't know" (or "uncertain") or to omit that option. Fifth, we had to choose a scale model and to fix an acceptable approximation to it. Thus, at each stage we had to decide in favor of some procedures and against others.

Defining the content domain broadly as items appearing in tests of morale and the like was based on the assumption that such items in the aggregate had relatively few dimensions and that each could be reliably represented by a scale. Our decision to list items from tests with a traceable link to the *American Journal of Sociology, American Sociological Review, Social Forces,* and *Sociometry* (now *Social Psychology Quarterly*), for the period 1960 to 1970 approximately, reflected our concern with measurement practice in sociology. The starting point of this research was the proliferation of ad hoc social life feeling scales in sociology (see Chapter One and Appendix A) and, correspondingly, the relative paucity of standard measures.

The 237 items for the sample survey questionnaire were selected from fourteen topical lists into which the master list of 545 items (Appendix B) had been divided. Our justification was that a sample selected in this manner would be more representative of the master list than a simple random sample. On most survey items, respondents were given a choice of "agree" or "disagree." Our justification was that (1) it takes less time to choose between two answers than three or more and (2) scores based on two-point answers are closely correlated with scores based on three-point answers or more.

In constructing scales, we required only that items have one factor in common. In symbols,

$$Y_i = a_i F + b_i U_i$$

We did not require that items consist of that common factor and nothing else. In symbols,

$$Y_i = a_i F$$

If we had imposed that restriction, we would have ended up with no scales, since responses to items almost always reflect a factor unique to each person.

But even with the less restricted model, we would have ended up with no scales if we had required literally that items have only one factor in common and nothing else. Accordingly, we had to relax that requirement or do without scales. Our decision to treat items as a scale if they had a Tucker-Lewis reliability coefficient of 0.90 represents a truce with reality. It allows for the presence of two or more common factors but still requires that 90 percent of the interitem correlation be attributable to one of them.

4

Comparing Social Life
Feeling Scales
to Other Measures

In this chapter, we consider the relation of the twelve SLFSs to
author scales, topic scales, and subject-class scales, defined below.
Our main purpose in investigating these relations was to determine
whether the SLFSs were closely correlated with such scales and
whether such correlations lent support or called into question our
interpretations of what it was the SLFSs were measuring.

An author scale is a set of items appearing in a previously
constructed scale; an example is the five items making up Srole's
(1956) original scale. A topic scale is a set of items considered to be
on the same topic, such as a set of items mentioning or alluding to
trust. A subject scale is a set of assertions about the same subject—for
example, a set of assertions about self.

In discussing the relation of SLFSs to scales in a given
classification—author, topic, subject—we first give a little detail on
the scales in that classification and then discuss each SLFS in terms
of the scale in that classification having the highest correlation with
it. In thus limiting the analysis, our assumption was that a SLFS's

closest statistical relative (as gauged by the correlation coefficient) would throw most light on what it was that SLFS was measuring.

The question of how well the SLFSs represent the earlier scales from which they were derived and/or the content categories to which items had been assigned before scales were constructed is also answered by this analysis. Our general answer to this question is a good fit between the twelve SLFSs and the given composites (author scales) and a still better fit between the twelve SLFSs and scores based on items judged to be similar in content. To that degree, the twelve SLFSs are representative of the content domain from which they were derived.

Author Scales

An author scale consists of one or more items from a previously constructed scale. Practically all the 237 items in the survey questionnaire had appeared in one or more previously constructed scales, and many previously constructed questionnaires were present in the questionnaire. However, not all such scales were represented by the same number of items: some were represented by only one item, some by a half dozen or more.

For purposes of this analysis, we arbitrarily dropped all author scales with fewer than three items. This left us with thirty-one author scales. We list them in Table 7 by date of publication and number of survey items available for analysis. Each of these thirty-one author scales was correlated with every one of the SLFSs, and each of the twelve SLFSs was then reanalyzed in terms of whichever author scale had the highest correlation with it. In the following discussion, we consider the bearing of these correlations on the meaning of the SLFSs; it is a brief summary of what was actually a lengthy mental operation.

SLFS1 had its highest correlation (0.78) with Srole's (Robinson and Shaver, 1972) nine-item scale for measuring anomie. Three items were present in both scales. This comparison suggests that SLFS1 and Srole's nine-item scale are measuring either the same feeling or different but closely related feelings. On the level of verbal interpretation, they are measuring different feelings: Srole's scale, by definition, ranges from a feeling of self-to-other belongingness at

Table 7. Author Scales.

Date	Authors	Concept	No. of Items
1936	Rundquist-Sletto	Morale	11
1949	Cavan and others	Usefulness	5
1956	Srole 1	Anomia	5
1957	Rosenberg	Faith in people	3
1958	Cumming-Dean-Newell	Morale (positive thinking)	6
1960	Mizruchi	Anomia	5
1961	Dean	Social isolation	8
1961	Walker	Job morale	6
1962	Rosenberg	Depressive affect	4
1964	Neal-Seeman	Powerlessness	6
1965	Bradburn-Caplovitz	Negative feelings	8
1965	Bradburn-Caplovitz	Positive feelings	4
1965	Bradburn-Caplovitz	Worry	8
1965	McClosky-Schaar	Anomy	8
1965	Struening-Richardson	Perceived purposelessness	6
1965	Struening-Richardson	Alienation via rejection	11
1966	Rotter	Internal/external control	12
1966	Smith	Satisfaction	3
1966	Smith	Efficacy in public affairs	3
1967	Groat-Neal	Meaninglessness	4
1967	Groat-Neal	Social isolation	6
1967	Dohrenwend-Langner	Psychological symptom index	7
1967	Marx	Index of morale	3
1968	Aiken and others	Index of anomia	7
1969	Gurin and others	Personal control	3
1969	Kohn-Schooler	Anxiety	5
1969	Srole 2	Anomia	9
1971	Conklin	General alienation	6
1972	Jackman	Personal efficacy	3
1972	Pierce-Clark	Depression/satisfaction	7
1972	Sheppard-Herrick	Alienation	3

one end to a feeling of self-to-other alienation at the other. We took SLFS1 to be a measure of the feeling that the American creed of individualism, or at least some of its tenets, does not square with one's own personal experiences—the feeling of discrepancy between the theoretical and actual importance of individual effort and initiative.

An interdependency between feelings of anomie and skepticism about individualism would account for the correlation between Srole's scale and SLFS1. It is plausible that doubts about the validity of individualism rise in proportion to the quantity of social failures. Persons who feel left out (a symptom of anomie) are likely to blame the system; persons who feel themselves to be very much a part of things are likely to credit themselves with their apparent social success. Such a mutual relation between the feeling of alienation from others and skepticism about the importance of individual effort could account for the correlation between SLFS1 and Srole's anomie scale.

SLFS2—initially called "Social Distrust"—had its highest correlation (0.77) with scores based on three items from Rosenberg's scale for measuring faith in people. One item was common to both scales.

From this moderately high correlation, and the similarity of content generally, we concluded that these scales were measuring closely similar feelings, if not exactly the same feeling. At the same time, since *social distrust* and *faith in people* differ somewhat in their connotations, we asked ourselves whether SLFS2 might not be better named "Faith in People." After reviewing content, we decided against that change; however, at this stage we did adopt the title "Trustworthiness of People." This revised title seemed to sumarize better our interpretation of SLFS2 as a measure of the respondent's doubt about the integrity and honesty of people generally.

SLFS3—Feeling Down—had its highest correlation (0.84) with scores based on Bradburn and Caplovitz's list of eight negative self-feelings. This list of eight has since come to be known as Bradburn's Negative Affect Scale, and we generally refer to it by that title. Despite their nominal difference, our SLFS3 and Bradburn's Negative Affect Scale are probably equivalent measures of the same trait, whatever it is. We prefer the everyday expression *feeling down* to the more technical term *negative affect*.

We note in passing that our statistical sorting of items led to the same conclusion that Bradburn came to by less formal methods—namely, that self-feeling scores should be based on positively worded items or negatively worded items but not both. Bradburn's theorizing about psychological well-being is based in part on the relation between positive and negative self-feeling scores.

SLFS4—originally called "Worker Morale"—had its highest correlation (0.67) with scores based on six items from Walker's questionnaire on morale in the British civil service. One of SLFS4's items came from Walker's set of six (part of a longer questionnaire). Nothing in this comparison argued for a revision of our interpretation of SLFS4 as a measure of job satisfaction. We interpreted SLFS4 as a measure of that feeling, and its statistically closest author scale was made up of items on worker morale—a concept that has job satisfaction as one of its connotations.

SLFS5—Faith in Citizen Involvement—had its highest correlation (0.78) with scores based on three items from Smith's questionnaire for gauging the feeling of efficacy in public affairs; all three of Smith's items were present in SLFS5. These results suggested that SLFS5 might better be named "Efficacy in Public Affairs."

In evaluating this possibility, we noted that all items in SLFS5, save one (No. 138), implied a discrepancy between citizen participation in fact and in theory—the way it is and the way it is supposed to be. Citizen involvement should make a difference, but it doesn't; people should have some say in government, but they don't. If our items collectively represent the feeling that participation does make a difference in the quality of government, then scores based on them might just as well be entitled "Faith in Citizen Involvement." It may be, and probably is, that faith in political involvement and the feeling of efficacy in public affairs are practically the same; however, the content of SLFS5 appears to pertain more immediately to citizen involvement than to a feeling of efficacy in public affairs.

SLFS6—Feeling Up—had its highest correlation (0.72) with scores based on four items from Rosenberg's scale for measuring depressive affect. Two of Rosenberg's four items were present in SLFS6. After reviewing content, we concluded that "Depressive Affect" would be something of a misnomer for SLFS6. Eight of SLFS6's eleven items afford the respondent a chance to present a picture of self as feeling up (rather than down), and scores based on these items correspond to the frequency of such self-presentations. It may be that not feeling up is a concomitant of feeling depressed; but that is a factual question. In any event, the everyday concept of feeling up (or feeling upbeat) seems to be more appropriate for SLFS6 than the more technical term *depressive affect*. We note in passing that SLFS6 is a companion to SLFS3. SLFS3, with all negative self-feelings, is an index of feeling down, whereas SLFS6, with positively directed items in the majority (eight of eleven), is an index of feeling up.

SLFS7—People Cynicism—had its highest correlation (0.80) with six items from Struening and Richardson's scale for measuring perceived purposelessness—something these authors regard as an aspect of alienation. Three items were present in both scales. These findings suggest that these scales may be measuring the same feeling and that SLFS7, which we took as a measure of people cynicism, might better be named "Perceived Purposelessness."

After reviewing items, we concluded that "People Cynicism" was probably the more appropriate title for SLFS7 and the mental attitude it reflected. Its items had two main themes: (1) people are generally aimless (do not know what they want) and (2) people are generally insincere (pretend to be what they are not). People are portrayed as having no well-defined goals in life and as acting for personal advantage rather than for the social good. Since that perception of human behavior comes close to the dictionary definition of *cynicism*, we decided in favor of "People Cynicism" over "Perceived Purposelessness."

SLFS8—Disillusionment with Government—had its highest correlation (0.61) with Srole's five-item scale for measuring anomia. One item was present in both scales. Despite this moderately high correlation, SLFS8 and Srole anomia are quite different in content and appear to be measuring different feelings, insofar as latent traits can be judged from the face of the items. As noted elsewhere, the Srole items portray the modern human being as existing in a social void with few close personal ties, whereas SLFS8's items present people as being generally cynical about the political process. Whether one regards such cynicism as an aspect of anomia will depend on how broadly one defines anomia—it might be stretched to include it. But however that problem is resolved, *political cyni-*

cism or *disillusionment with government* is more descriptive of the content of SLFS8 than *anomia*.

We note again that SLFS8 is a companion to SLFS5. Both reflect a disenchantment with key articles of political democracy—citizen participation and trustworthy officials. The difference between them lies mainly in the direction of their items.

SLFS9—Future Outlook—had its highest correlation (0.75) with scores based on eleven items from Rundquist and Sletto's questionnaire for measuring morale. Three items were present in both sets. In their work, Rundquist and Sletto were expressly concerned with the mental attitude of people during the economic depression of the 1930s—whether people were generally hopeful and optimistic (in spite of economic hardship) or filled with despair and given to pessimism. They called that feeling "morale." We took SLFS9 to be a reflection of one's outlook on the future: rosy, hopeful, promising, at one extreme; hopeless, gloomy, and foreboding, at the other. Perhaps it is immaterial whether the feeling of hopelessness (or hopefulness) is called "morale" or "future outlook." The term *future outlook* carries no connotation of giving up, as the term *morale* might, and for that reason we chose this somewhat broader concept for the feeling we took SLFS9 to be measuring.

Of all twelve scales, *SLFS10*—Economic Self-Determination—was alone in having no relatively close relative among the thirty-one author scales. Its highest correlation (0.28) was with scores based on five items from Struening and Richardson's list for measuring alienation via rejection. (Struening and Richardson, 1965, proposed two measures of alienation.) One of these five items appeared in SLFS10.

In respect to SLFS10's uniqueness: It is possible that SLFS10 had relatively high correlations with scales present in the entire domain but not present in our group of thirty-one author scales with three or more items. Or it may be that no scale in the domain had a high correlation with SLFS10. In this latter event, SLFS10 could be pointing to a previously overlooked and unmeasured social life feeling; in the former, it would simply be pointing to an already recognized social life feeling that was not represented by any of the thirty-one tests, a possibility we regard as the more likely.

SLFS11—Feeling Demoralized—had its highest correlation (0.62) with scores based on three items from Gurin's questionnaire on personal control. (This questionnaire was based on a factor analysis of Rotter's twenty-two-item scale for measuring internal/external control.) One of Gurin's items appeared in SLFS11.

SLFS11 did not lend itself readily to analysis in terms of the content of Gurin, partly because of differences in length—Gurin had three items, SLFS11 had nine. The moderately high correlation did suggest that the feeling of demoralization was related in some degree to the feeling of having little or no control over external events. However, insofar as one can judge from the face of the items, SLFS11 seems to reflect more the feeling of demoralization than the feeling that circumstances are beyond one's control, and we decided, therefore, that morale (feeling demoralized) was a more apt concept for this scale than the feeling of little or no control.

SLFS12—Career Concerns—had its highest correlation (0.83) with scores based on eight items from Bradburn and Caplovitz's list of ten worries. Five of these eight appeared in SLFS12. A natural question is why three of the eight items did not appear. The answer is that these eight items (as shown by factor analysis) fell into two distinct clusters, the one made up of items on making it socially and economically, the other of items on getting old and dying. In screening items for homogeneity, the items on health and old age dropped out, leaving us with items on getting ahead, or not falling behind. SLFS12 thus emerged, not as a measure of tendency to worry in general, but rather as an index of concern about making it socially and economically—what might be called a concern for level of social performance. SLFS12 should accordingly be viewed not as a short form of the Bradburn-Caplovitz worry questionnaire but rather as a theme-specific form.

Topic Scales

As noted elsewhere (Appendix B), the 237 items in our questionnaire had been selected in stages from a pool of about 1,000 items appearing in over 100 tests of feelings (as defined) toward self or others in society; however, before choosing items we had grouped them by topical similarity, with the idea of representing every main topic in the survey questionnaire by twenty items or so, split equally between keys (agree and disagree). Owing to differences in both the number of items within topics and their division between keys, it was not possible to adhere strictly to this plan. In the "final 237," keys were not equally represented within topics, nor were topics equally represented within keys.

However, for present purposes it was possible to set up key-balanced topic scales by dropping items from whichever key had the larger number. Then, for key-uniform topic scales, we merely split the key-balanced scales. On analyzing the longer key-balanced scales, we discovered what we might have anticipated, namely, that practically every such scale had two common factors—a content factor and a direction-of-wording (key) factor. In view of this complication, we decided to limit the analysis to correlations between SLFSs and key-uniform topic scales. There were 324 such correlations: twenty-seven for each of the twelve SLFSs, or twelve for each of the twenty-seven key-uniform scales.

Comparing key-uniform scales within topics permitted us to judge the importance of direction of wording with topic controlled; comparing topic scales within keys permitted us to gauge the importance of topic with key controlled. Our main finding on this point was that although differences between correlations within topics were substantial, they were generally smaller than differences among correlations within keys. This finding is an indication that the correlation between a given SLFS and a given topic scale depends not only on similarity of content but on similarity in direction of wording (key) as well.

However, our primary interest was not in this methodological issue but rather in the light the topic scales might throw on whatever it was the SLFSs were measuring. With that object in mind, we again reviewed what each SLFS was measuring but now in terms of whichever topic scale had the highest correlation with it.

Three scales were closest to the topic of self-determination: SLFS1 had its highest correlation (0.83) with ten negative statements on that topic; SLFS11 had its highest correlation (0.63) with the same ten; SLFS10 had its highest correlation (0.74) with ten positive statements. None of these correlations was at odds with scale interpretations as first drawn.

The highest correlations for Nos. 2, 4, 5 and 8 were also in line with scale interpretations: SLFS2 had its highest correlation

(0.75) with nine negative items on trust; SLFS4 had its highest correlation (0.85) with ten negative statements on work morale; SLFS5 had its best correlation (0.85) with ten positive statements on civic morale; SLFS8 had its best correlation (0.81) with ten negative statements on the same topic.

SLFS3 (Feeling Down) had its highest correlation with élan, and SLFS6 (Feeling Up) had its highest correlation with dejection. One might have predicted the opposite. The explanation is that élan and dejection are incomplete captions. Items expressing apathy (opposite to élan) were assigned to élan, and items expressing elation (opposite to dejection) were assigned to dejection. It was actually the reverse side of élan that was correlated with SLFS3, and the reverse side of dejection that was correlated with SLFS6. Best correlations were thus not inconsistent with scale interpretations.

SLFS7 had its highest correlation (0.55) with six negative items on expediency, defined as the tendency of individuals to advance themselves personally regardless of the consequences. The relatively low correlation between people cynicism and expediency gave us pause, and to explain it we carefully reexamined the contents of both sets. Our conclusion was that SLFS7 included items not only on expediency, as we had construed that term, but also on the aimlessness of people. The items making up SLFS7 cast doubt on both the motives of people and the firmness of their aims and goals. For that reason, the term *people cynicism* seems to describe better the feeling indexed by SLFS7 than *expediency*.

SLFS9—Future Outlook—had its highest correlation (0.80) with scores based on twelve negative statements on social optimism. Since we had included items expressive of the tendency to be either cheerful or gloomy about the future under social optimism, this comparison was not out of line with our interpretation of SLFS9 as an index of one's feeling about the future. It is of interest that the correlation of SLFS9 and twelve positive items on optimism was appreciably smaller—0.51—suggesting that SLFS9 is more a measure of pessimism than optimism; that is to say, it reflects more the tendency to take a bleak view of the future than the tendency to take a bright view.

SLFS12—Career Concerns—had its highest correlation (0.82) with ten items on common worries (Bradburn and Caplovitz's list of eight plus two from other sources). Since the list of ten includes the six making up SLFS12, no substantive significance should be attached to what amounts to a part-whole correlation. It is of interest, from the standpoint of scale construction, that the longer scale of ten had an alpha reliability of 0.57 and a Tucker-Lewis homogeneity of 0.52, whereas the shorter (screened) list of six (SLFS12) had an alpha reliability of 0.65 and a Tucker-Lewis reliability of 0.91. In this case, *both* reliabilities were improved by dropping items, contrary to the general experience.

Subject Classes

In reviewing the final questionnaire of 237 items, but before giving it to the national sample (Appendix C), we noticed that many items were either assertions about self or assertions about society. Of items about self, some answered to the question of how the respondent feels, some called for an evaluation of one's own situation, and some seemed to express a personal philosophy of life. Of items about society, some were about people collectively and some were about social institutions. This observation suggested to us that the correlation between items might be due to similarity of subject as well as to similarity of content.

To pursue this matter, we had six judges (Ph.D. students in sociology) classify 227 items according to whether they expressed (1) a personal feeling (I feel good); (2) an evaluation of one's own situation (I am satisfied with my job); (3) a personal philosophy of life (honesty is the best policy); (4) an opinion about people collectively (people cannot be trusted); or (5) an opinion about social institutions (newspapers are unreliable). As a convenience, we refer to these categories as subject classes and denote them SC1, SC2, SC3, SC4, and SC5.

The six judges were in perfect (6 to 0) agreement on 113 items; in good (5 to 1) agreeement on 44 items; in fair (4 to 2) agreement on 35 items; and in poor (no subject class more than 3 votes) agreement on 35 items. (For detail, see Schuessler and Wallace, 1979.)

To investigate the relation between the twelve SLFSs and the classification of items by subject class, we first counted the items on which there was perfect, good, fair, and poor agreement, respectively, within scales; second, we tallied the number of votes by subject class within scales; and third, we correlated SLFSs with scores based on key-uniform items from the same object class. In setting up these scores, we first dropped all items with fewer than five votes in one subject class—items on which there was less than good agreement—and then selected ten agree-keyed and ten disagree-keyed items from each subject class. Subsequently, by reason that scores based on eight items were almost perfectly correlated with scores based on ten, we dropped the two least useful items from each set and carried out the final analysis on sets of eight items apiece.

The most common pattern of findings within SLFSs was good agreement between judges or better on a majority of items; a heavy concentration of votes in a single subject class; and a moderately high correlation with scores based on key-specific items from the same subject class. Here is the detail.

Judges were in poor agreement on seven of SLFS1's fourteen items, and votes were scattered among four of the five subject classes, but not evenly. Subject class 3 received the largest number of votes, thirty-four of eighty-four, and, consistent with this, SLFS1 had its highest correlation (0.75) with scores based on negatively worded items from that subject class (SC3A). These findings indicate that items may approximate criteria scale even though they differ in their subject classes (as judged).

There was no disagreement among judges on SLFS2's items, and all items fell in subject class 4. Consistent with this, SLFS2 had its highest correlation (0.86) with scores based on items from that subject class. These findings suggest that in some cases it may be necessary to eliminate subject-class differences between items in order to meet scale criteria.

There was perfect agreement on nine of the ten items making up SLFS3 and good agreement on the tenth item. With a single exception, all votes fell into subject class 1. Consistent with this pattern, SLFS3 had its highest correlation (0.90) with scores based on items from that subject class (SC1A). Here, as with SLFS2, it appears that subject-class differences were eliminated in the process of screening items for acceptable levels of reliability.

In the case of SLFS4, judges were in fair agreement or better on all nine items, and practically all votes fell in subject class 2. In line with this concentration, SLFS4 had its highest correlation (0.79) with negatively worded items from this subject class (SC2A).

Judges were in perfect agreement on seven of ten items in SLFS5, and all seven were in subject class 5; two of the remaining three items showed fair agreement or better. Since votes were concentrated in subject class 5, we expected that SLFS5 would have its highest correlation with scores based on items from that subject class. A correlation of 0.72 with scores based on negative assertions from that subject class (SC5A) bore out this prediction.

Judges showed poor consensus on five of eleven items making up SLFS6, and votes were necessarily scattered among several classes. Subject class 2 had a plurality of two votes over subject class 1, but the latter had the highest correlation (0.51) with SLFS6. This comparison suggests that items about self may form a scale, even though they differ in their contextual specificity.

Judges were in perfect agreement on SLFS7's items, and all items fell in subject class 4. Consistent with this finding, SLFS7 had its highest correlation (0.66) with scores based on items from that subject class (SC4A).

Judges were in good agreement or better on all items in SLFS8, and all items were practically identical in their classification. Subject class 5 drew over 90 percent of all votes, and in line with this pattern, SLFS8 had its highest correlation (0.90) with scores based on items from this subject class (SC5A).

Judges tended to agree on SLFS9's items; however, the items differed among themselves in their subject classes. Subject class 4 received the largest number of votes (but only a bare majority), and SLFS9 had its highest correlation (0.69) with scores based on items from that subject class (SC4A).

In the case of SLFS10, as in SLFS9, there was agreement among judges on individual items but differences among items in their subject classes. Subject class 3 had the largest number of votes (but not a majority), and SLFS10 had its highest correlation (0.33) with scores based on five positively worded items from that subject class.

The vote pattern for SLFS11 reflected a lack of consensus of judges on individual items—five of nine showed poor agreement. Subject class 1 received the largest number of votes (but not quite a majority), and SLFS11 had its highest correlation (0.60) with scores based on items drawn from that subject class (SC1D).

By oversight, the items forming SLFS12 were omitted from the list of items presented to judges. It is not unreasonable that all six might have been placed in subject class 2, since all items refer to personal concern about some practical social endeavor—marriage, work, children, and so on. An implication is that SLFS12 would have its highest correlation with scores based on items from that subject class. Contrary to expectation, SLFS12 had its highest correlation (0.13) with scores based on items from subject class 4—assertions about people. This highest correlation indicates that SLFS12 was generally uncorrelated with subject-class scales.

By pairing highest SLFS-SCS correlation with vote percentage in same subject class, it is possible to discern the tendency of these two series to covary. Table 8 shows those pairings. This display shows that the two series do tend to move together but that this tendency is only moderately strong and there are exceptions. For example, all of the votes on the items in SLFS7 went to subject class 4, but the correlation of SLFS7 and scores based on items from that subject class was only moderately large—0.66. However, SLFS1, with an only moderate concentration of votes in subject class 3, had a correlation of 0.75 with scores based on items in that subject class.

This latter case, as an exception, is a reminder that a SLFS need not consist solely of items from the same subject class; at the same time, it draws attention to the general rule that SLFSs usually consist of items from the same subject class (as here defined).

Comparing Classifications

Since all scales—social life feeling, author, topic, subject class—were based on the same list of items, we expected them to be

Table 8. Highest SLFS-SCS Correlation and Percentage Votes in Same Subject Class.

SLFS	3	8	2	4	1	5	9	7	11	6	10	12
SCS	1A	5A	4A	2A	3A	5D	4A	4A	1D	1D	3D	4D
Corr.	90	90	86	79	75	72	69	66	60	51	33	13
% Votes	98	94	100	83	40	80	53	100	49	41	47	

correlated with one another to a greater or lesser degree. And this overlap within and between categories raised the possibility that some scales were redundant and might be reasonably represented by others and the related possibility that a relatively small number of scales might serve to represent the entire lot of eighty (twelve SLFSs, thirty-one author scales, twenty-seven topic scales, ten subject-class scales).

For an answer to this question, we proceeded as follows: we defined two scales as representative of each other, but not equally so, if they had a correlation larger than 0.60; and within such pairs, we took as the more representative whichever scale had the higher relia-bility. Given these definitions, our problem was to ascertain which scales could not be represented at all; which scales could be repre-sented by one or more other scales; and, of this latter group, which scales would do the representing, or which scales would serve on behalf of one or more other scales.

Scales that could not be represented at all were simply (by definition) those scales with no correlation larger than 0.60. There were nine such scales.

Scales that could be represented were scales having at least one correlation larger than 0.60. There were seventy-one such scales—the total number (eighty) less the number that could not be represented at all (nine). To identify the most representative of these seventy-one, we dropped from each pair of scales whichever one had the lower alpha reliability. At the end of this screening, we had dropped sixty scales and kept eleven. No two of these eleven scales had a correlation of 0.60 or larger with each other, and each had a correlation larger than 0.60 with at least one of the discarded scales.

Here are the eleven surviving scales and the number of scales displaced by each:

SLFS1	16
SLFS2	14
SLFS3	7
SLFS4	5
SLFS5	8
SLFS6	5
SLFS9	11
SLFS10	1
SLFS12	2
McClosky-Schaar	1
Topic 11(P)	1

The representativeness of a given scale may be gauged by the number of scales dropped in its favor, or the number of proxies assigned to it. By this criterion, SLFS1, with sixteen displacements, is most representative, and Topic 11(P), SLFS10, and McClosky-Schaar, with one apiece, are least representative.

It is relevant that nine of the eleven most representative scales are SLFSs. It would thus appear that the statistically constructed scales serve best to represent a mixed lot of author, topic, subject-class, and SLFS scales, excluding those scales with no correlation in excess of 0.60. However, this outcome was an almost foregone conclusion, given the composition of our domain and our method of scale construction. Our domain consisted of items that tended to cluster by reason of topic and subject class, and our method of scale construction tended to restore these clusters.

Summary Points

It is fair to ask what we learned about the twelve SLFSs by examining them in relation to scales in different categories—author, topic, subject class. We answer that question by first summarizing and discussing findings for each of the three categories separately and then for all three categories combined.

Author Scales. Every SLFS had a correlation of 0.60 or higher with one or more author scales except SLFS10. On comparing what we took the SLFSs (disregarding SLFS10) to be measuring with what it was their closest author scales had been devised to measure, we found little or no difference in four cases, after making an allowance for differences in terminology. In those seven cases in which a difference existed, we reexamined the contents of the SLFSs to determine whether our interpretation should perhaps be revised. In two cases (SLFS 1 and 2), we made minor modifications, and with the other five we let our original interpretation stand. The object of this exercise was to arrive at a more accurate statement of just what it was that our SLFSs were measuring.

Topic Scales. Every SLFS had a correlation of 0.60 or higher with one or more topic scales, with one exception. On comparing what we took the SLFSs to be measuring with what the statistically closest topic scales apparently expressed, we generally found only minor differences. In the case of SLFS7, where a major difference in interpretation seemed to exist, no revision was required, since the correlation was relatively low (0.55).

Although our main concern was the meaning of SLFSs from the standpoint of topic scales, at the same time we wondered whether topic scales were equal to the SLFSs in meeting scale criteria. As a group, they were inferior to the SLFSs; individually, they differed widely in meeting scale criteria.

Subject-Class Scales. The finding that the best correlations—one for each SLFS—tended to decrease as degree of overlap in subject-class composition decreased was in accord with our original hunch that items between statistically constructed scales would probably differ in their subject classes, while items within scales would be alike. That hunch was contradicted by several negative cases: in one case (SLFS7) there was 100 percent overlap in subject-class composition but a relatively low correlation; in two cases (SLFSs 5 and 9) there was relatively little overlap in subject-class composition but a moderately high correlation. These exceptions do not prove the general rule; they merely indicate that items from different subject classes may approximate a one-factor scale.

As with topic scales, we asked whether subject-class scales more nearly approximated scale criteria than SLFSs. As a group, they were below the SLFSs in their reliabilities; individually, some were well above the minimum requirements, while others were far below.

Combined Findings. The combined findings suggest that controls on direction of wording and subject class may be necessary to approximate one-factor SLFSs. At least in screening for such scales, we ended up with items that were similar in direction of wording and subject class, as well as in topic, or meaning. Of course, the match between the twelve SLFSs and items grouped by topic, subject class, and direction of wording was not perfect. In the case of job satisfaction (SLFS4), direction of wording seemed to make little difference; in the case of doubt about individualism (SLFS1), subject class made relatively little difference. Nevertheless, in the main, items tended to arrange themslves into groupings that were similar in topic, direction of wording, and subject class. This finding is the basic of our conclusion that controls on direction of wording and subject class may be required in order to approximate one-factor social life feeling scales.

Limitations. The findings reported herein would undoubtedly change somewhat if we were to change our topic, subject-class, and direction-of-wording classifications, respectively. For example, if we were to scale items by the method of equal-appearing intervals instead of merely classifying them as positive or negative, we might find that SLFSs consisted of items with high scales values, low scale values, or middle values, but never both high and low values together. By this technique, we might discover more precisely just what is necessary in respect to directionality if items are to conform to one-factor scales.

Or if we were to classify items by subject as noun or pronoun, and within each of these speech parts as plural or singular, we might get some further insight into why items closely similar in content on their face nevertheless tend to fall into different SLFSs. And by this technique generally we might discover just what is required by way of syntactical (and possibly idiomatic) similarity if items are to form one-factor social life feeling scales. From this point of view, the findings of this chapter are significant not only in demonstrating that subject class and direction of wording are significant in scale homogeneity but also in pointing to a probably fruitful line of study.

5

How Social Background
Influences
People's Responses

In this chapter we consider the relation of the twelve SLFSs to age, race, income, education, and marital status. Since social life feelings presumably reflect the content of social experience, and since social experience is contingent on such factors as age and education, it is plausible that social categories would differ in their social life feeling scores.

The questionnaire included thirty-one background questions (see Appendix B), but not every question applied to every respondent. Some applied only to those regularly employed, some only to those presently married, and so forth. However, the applicability of a question to all or some played no part in our decision to limit this discussion to age, race, income, education, and marital status.

In analyzing the relation of the twelve SLFSs to the various social and demographic factors, we discovered that the largest two-factor coefficient of determination, or percentage explained variance (PEV), could seldom be raised by adding variables; that is to say, three-factor multiple correlations or higher were seldom larger by statistically significant increments than two-factor multiple correla-

73

tions. Furthermore, the largest two-factor correlations were generally based on a combination of age, race, income, education, and marital status, two at a time. That finding is our principal justification for limiting this presentation to those particular factors.

In thus limiting the discussion, we risk conveying the false impression that these five classifications are theoretically important because they are statistically efficient. But theoretical importance has nothing to do with statistical efficiency: that will depend on the substantive hypothesis being tested. If the influence of religion on a particular social life feeling is in question, then the relation of religion to that social feeling would be considered. One might even propose a structural model specifying the effect of religion on a given social life feeling via one or more intervening variables, as well as a possible direct effect. This remark is simply a reminder that the relevance of a factor in a given problem will depend not on its statistical efficiency but rather on the sociological hypothesis being investigated.

But whatever the theoretical importance of age, race, income, education, and marital status, if any, they do serve best (in our sample) for predicting SLFS scores in the sense of maximizing the between-groups (social background) variance. They may point to the conditions of social life that have the greatest effect on social life feelings.

Moreover, they yield relatively reliable measures, simply and cheaply: reliable, because they pertain to objective characteristics of the individual—age, years of schooling, and so on; simply, because the questions on which they are based apply to all respondents and require little explanation in their administration; and cheaply, because these same questions take little time to answer. For these practical reasons, information on these factors might be routinely collected whenever any social life feeling scale is given, even though the exact use of that information is unknown at the time.

Class Means

In this section, we give class means by age, race, income, education, and marital status for each of the twelve SLFSs. These averages are given in Table 9; also given are the percentage (propor-

Table 9. Class Means and Proportion Explained Variance, Twelve SLFSs.

Classification	N	SLFS 1	2	3	4	5	6	7	8	9	10	11	12
Age													
18–29	(400)	5.21	4.43	3.68	3.23	5.92	3.02	4.32	4.97	6.86	1.94	2.02	4.73
30–44	(441)	4.95	3.74	3.01	1.94	5.14	2.73	3.87	4.52	6.52	1.66	1.99	4.97
45–59	(448)	5.99	3.84	2.83	1.85	5.27	2.98	3.91	5.07	7.01	1.52	2.51	3.92
60+	(225)	7.44	3.89	3.08	1.64	5.40	3.79	3.89	5.36	8.04	1.48	3.73	2.78
PEV		.055	.012	.016	.078	.015	.017	.015	.014	.024	.020	.089	.227
Race													
White	(1298)	5.34	3.74	3.06	2.27	5.46	2.91	3.93	4.81	6.86	1.63	2.23	4.23
Nonwhite[a]	(221)	7.79	5.38	3.65	2.43	5.23	3.71	4.47	5.61	7.63	1.85	3.41	4.47
PEV		.059	.054	.006	.001	.001	.012	.014	.014	.008	.004	.044	.003
Family income													
Under $8,000	(521)	7.27	4.64	3.72	2.66	5.68	3.95	4.28	5.42	7.86	1.83	3.26	3.92
$8,000–12,000	(300)	5.59	3.98	3.14	2.29	5.21	2.78	3.92	4.90	7.03	1.62	2.20	4.41
Over $12,000	(522)	4.06	3.29	2.59	2.15	5.30	2.20	3.79	4.41	5.99	1.55	1.59	4.60
PEV		.157	.057	.035	.009	.006	.094	.019	.034	.070	.010	.142	.038
Education													
Less than 12 years	(549)	7.77	4.81	3.77	2.34	5.79	3.72	4.20	5.69	8.15	1.68	3.52	3.85
12 years	(495)	5.59	3.77	2.97	2.55	5.31	2.78	3.89	4.73	6.81	1.50	2.02	4.49
More than 12 years	(463)	4.06	3.19	2.58	2.01	5.01	2.48	3.89	4.21	5.74	1.83	1.47	4.52
PEV		.228	.073	.035	.011	.014	.044	.009	.066	.100	.011	.196	.040
Marital status													
Married	(991)	5.32	3.83	2.88	2.13	5.36	2.62	3.91	4.80	6.82	1.59	2.66	4.44
Widowed	(181)	6.90	3.83	3.36	1.73	5.38	3.99	3.89	5.28	7.60	1.63	3.43	3.23
Divorced	(155)	6.96	4.61	4.03	2.25	5.58	4.26	4.47	5.31	7.52	1.93	2.90	4.55
Single	(191)	4.33	5.48	3.54	1.34	5.73	3.23	4.21	4.86	6.68	1.82	2.33	4.16
PEV		.034	.003	.025	.032	.004	.055	.014	.008	.015	.010	.046	.065
Two-factor PEV (largest)		.280	.109	.066	.097	.034	.110	.035	.076	.119	.033	.252	.238

[a]Black, 184; other, 37.

tion) explained variance (PEV) for each factor for each scale and the largest two-factor PEV for each scale.

For each scale, after briefly restating its interpretation, we comment on differences between means within classifications (for example, differences between marital status categories) and on differences between classifications in predictive efficiency (for example, whether age is more efficient than marital status in predicting individual scores).

The class means of Table 9 are unadjusted means. They may be adjusted in various ways (by an analysis of variance), and we carried out many such calculations. For example, we calculated score means for age groups with marital status and race held constant. Whereas adjusted and unadjusted means almost always differed in their magnitudes within classifications, adjusted and unadjusted PEVs seldom differed in their rank orders between classifications. Thus, the effect of race relative to education was not reversed upon controlling both on age, income, and marital status. As a rule, zero-order PEVs and corresponding partial PEVs had the same rank order.

SLFS1. Higher and lower scores on this scale correspond to stronger and weaker doubts about self-determination. Nonwhites scored higher than whites; persons with less income scored higher than persons with more income; persons with less schooling scored higher than persons with more schooling. By age, the oldest had the highest mean score; and by marital status, the divorced and the separated had the highest mean score.

Education had the largest PEV (22.8); income was next at 15.7, followed by race, age, and marital status, in that order. Education and income had the largest two-factor PEV (28.0), which was, incidentally, the largest for all twelve scales.

Although none of the above statistics demonstrates causality, all are more or less in line with sociological expectation. We would expect, for example, that persons who are above average in income and education would be less inclined to doubt the importance of personal drive and perseverance than persons who are below average in those classifications.

SLFS2. High scorers feel that people are less trustworthy than low scorers. By age, the youngest had the highest mean score; among marital groupings, the divorced and separated had the highest average score. Respondents with less education had a higher average than respondents with more; persons with smaller incomes had a higher average than persons with larger incomes. Nonwhites scored higher, on the average, than whites.

Education had the largest PEV at 7.3 and marital status the smallest at 0.3. Income and race were about equal at 5.0, and age was just slightly larger than 1.0. Education and race together accounted for 10.9 percent of the score variance—the largest two-factor PEV.

SLFS3. Higher and lower scores on this scale correspond to higher and lower degrees of feeling down. Nonwhites scored higher than whites; persons with smaller incomes scored higher than persons with larger incomes; persons with less schooling scored higher than persons with more schooling. By age, the youngest scored highest; and by marital status, the divorced had the highest mean score.

Education and income each contributed 3.5 percent to the score variation, followed in order by marital status, age, and race. Education and age together contributed 6.6 percent to the variation in scores for the largest two-factor PEV. Generally speaking, score differences on SLFS3 are not closely correlated with age, race, income, education, or marital status. One might say that these factors exert an only negligible effect on what has come to be known as negative affect.

SLFS4. This scale is a measure of job satisfaction, answering to the question of how the worker feels about his or her job—its tangible and intangible rewards. By age, the youngest had the highest mean score (lowest job satisfaction); and by marital status, the divorced had the highest mean score. Nonwhites scored higher than whites, and persons under $12,000 in income scored higher than persons over that figure. By education, respondents with just high school had the highest average score.

Age had the largest PEV (7.8) and marital status the second largest (3.2). Education was just above 0.1, and both income and race were below that level. Age and education together had the largest two-factor PEV, about two points higher than age alone. It is of interest that income, as measured, appears to make little difference in job satisfaction.

SLFS5. This scale reflects feelings about citizen involvement in government—whether it is worthwhile and important (low scoring) or hardly worth the time and trouble (high scoring). Nonwhites scored higher than whites (had more doubts about involvement); among income groups, respondents with the smallest incomes had the highest mean score; and among educational groups, respondents with the fewest years of schooling had the highest average score. By marital status, single persons had the highest mean score.

Perhaps the most significant finding is the relative uniformity of scores across background categories, or the absence of correlation between scores and background factors. With one exception, all one-factor PEVs were smaller than 2.0, and the largest two-factor PEV (age and education) was 3.4. It thus appears that SLFS5, however interpreted, is only weakly related to age, race, income, education, and marital status.

SLFS6. Lower measures on this scale correspond to feeling up, higher measures correspond to not feeling up. Nonwhites had a higher mean score than whites; persons with less income had a higher mean score than persons with more income; persons with less education had a higher mean than persons with more education. By age, persons over sixty years had the highest mean score; by marital status, the divorced had the highest mean.

Income had the largest one-factor PEV (9.4) and marital status the next largest; education was third largest. As with SLFS3, race and age made very little difference statistically. Income and marital status had the largest two-factor PEV (11.1)—not much larger than income alone.

We expected SLFS3 and SLFS6 to be closely similar in background relations, since they were so similar in verbal content. Their background relations were similar but not identical: income and marital status ranked higher on SLFS6 than on SLFS3, while education ranked lower. By and large, SLFS6 showed more correlation with age, race, education, income, and marital status than did SLFS3. In our sample, feeling up, or positive affect, is more dependent (statistically) on socioeconomic background than negative affect, or feeling down.

SLFS7. This scale expresses the idea that persons are moved not by purpose and principle but rather by considerations of self-advantage. The higher the score, the stronger this feeling. Nonwhites scored higher than whites; persons of lower socioeconomic standing scored higher than persons of high standing. By age, the youngest grouping had the highest mean score (were most cynical about the motives of others); the divorced and separated had the highest mean among the marital categories.

Income had the largest PEV at 1.9 and age the next largest with 1.5; race and marital status were equal at 1.4; education contributed less than 1 percent to the score variance. Income and age had the largest two-factor PEV. In general, background factors were only weakly correlated with SLFS7. If particular social circumstances determine degree of cynicism, they evidently are not associated to any degree with age, race, income, education, or marital status.

SLFS8. This scale is an index of cynicism about politics and politicians, with higher scores reflecting more cynicism, lower scores less. Nonwhites scored higher than whites; respondents with less income scored higher than respondents with more; and respondents with less than high school scored higher than respondents with high school or more. By age, respondents over sixty years had the highest mean score; by marital status, the divorced and separated had the highest.

Education had the largest PEV at 6.6 and income the next largest at 3.4. The effects of marital status, age, and race were relatively small, none contributing more than 1.5 percent to the score variance. Education and income had the largest two-factor PEV, about twice as large as SLFS5's largest two-factor PEV. It will be recalled that SLFS5 and SLFS8 are companion scales.

SLFS9. This scale indexes one's outlook on the social future—what we here call "pessimism" as a convenience. Higher and lower scores correspond to more and less pessimism. Nonwhites were more pessimistic (had a higher average score) than whites, and respondents with less income and schooling were more pessimistic than respondents with more. Among age groups, the oldest were most pessimistic; among marital groups, the widowed were most pessimistic.

Education had the largest PEV, income the second largest, followed by age, marital status, and race, in that order. Education and income together accounted for 11.5 percent of the total variation in scores, just two points more than education alone. None of these findings is particularly surprising. It is not surprising that those who have shared least in what might be called the good life are the most pessimistic about the future.

SLFS10. This scale arrays individuals from low to high according to degree of doubt about economic self-determination. Persons scoring high express more doubts than persons scoring low. Older persons had fewer doubts (lower mean score) than younger persons; whites had fewer doubts than nonwhites. Among marital categories, the divorced and separated had the highest mean score; by income, persons at the lowest level had the highest mean score; by education, respondents with just high school (the middle grouping) had the lowest mean score, and persons with some college had the highest.

Age had the largest PEV at 2.0, and income, education, and marital status were almost equal in the vicinity of 1.0. The coefficient on race was just noticeably different from zero. The findings indicate that respondents in their twenties are somewhat more skeptical about the value of personal initiative than persons in the middle and later years.

SLFS11. Higher and lower scores on this scale correspond to stronger and weaker feelings of demoralization. Correlations between SLFS11 scores and background factors are similar to those for SLFS1, except that race is relatively less important, and the means for marital categories differ in their rank order. By age, respondents over sixty years had the highest mean score; by race, nonwhites were higher than whites; by marital status, the divorced and separated had the highest average score. As with SLFS1 (SLFS11's statistically closest SLFS), persons with smaller incomes had a higher mean score than persons with larger incomes, and persons with less schooling had a higher mean score than persons with more schooling.

Education and income had the largest and next-largest PEVs; at the other end, race had the smallest PEV, with marital status next smallest; age stood between marital status and income. The interpretation of SLFS11 as a measure of personal demoralization gets some support from the degree of its correlation with age. A variety of studies show that persons past the prime of life tend to become demoralized.

SLFS12. This scale indexes one's concern with social performance—getting ahead, earning money, raising children. Persons scoring high show more concern than persons scoring low. Nonwhites expressed more concern than whites; persons over $12,000 showed more concern than persons below that figure; persons with more education had a higher average score than persons with less education. By age, persons between thirty and forty-five years had the highest mean score; and by marital status, the divorced had the highest mean score.

Age had the largest PEV (22.7) by a wide margin; marital status was next at 6.5, followed by income and education at around 4.0; the coefficient on race was just noticeable. Age and marital status had the largest two-factor PEV (23.8), only a little larger than age alone. The results suggest generally that persons of higher socioeconomic status (other things equal) are more concerned about performing well as parent, spouse, breadwinner than persons of lower socioeconomic status.

General Conclusions

Several general conclusions may be drawn from the entries of Table 9, the more easily after they have been rearranged and tallied: First, the rank order of class means within factors (age, race, and so on) was fairly constant across all twelve scales; second, differences between class means, although almost always significant, seldom accounted for more than 10 percent of the score variance; third, while factors differed in degree of importance, no one factor had the largest PEV on every scale; fourth, scales similar in content are no more similar in their background relations than scales dissimilar in content.

1. The tendency of class means to occupy the same rank on every scale may be gauged by the number of times in 12 that class means had the same rank order. Here is the tally: age, 8; race, 11; income, 10; education, 9; marital status, 8. This tabulation shows that the rank of nonwhites relative to whites was the same on all scales but one; it indicates that the rank of one income class relative to another was the same on ten of the twelve scales, and analogously, on nine of the twelve scales for education. Rank orders for both age and marital status were the same on eight of the twelve

scales. The order of social classifications by degree of accuracy in predicting rank order of class means was thus race, income, education, and age and marital status. In view of the rather small differences between subgroup means, one might have predicted less constancy in their rank orders across scales.

2. For comparisons between class means, the usual result was a relatively small but statistically significant PEV. Almost half of all PEVs (twenty-nine of sixty) were smaller than 2.0 percent, and only six were larger than 10.0 percent. In general, PEVs were small. Nevertheless, of the entire lot of sixty, only four were lacking in significance (at the 5 percent level). These frequencies are the basis of our conclusion that background factors have a generally weak but statistically significant effect on SLFS scores.

3. No one factor always had the largest PEV, but some factors were more influential, on the average, than others. Factors differed on number of times in a given rank and also on mean rank. Table 10 shows the frequencies. Education had the highest rank, on the average (mean = 1.92), and the greatest influence on scores by that criterion; by the same criterion race, with the lowest average rank, had the least influence. Age had the largest PEV (rank 1) on four of the twelve SLFSs, but its overall effect was about the same as that of marital status. If we had to generalize, we would say that the social circumstances affecting SLFS scores, whatever they are, are more closely associated with income and education than with age, marital status, and race.

Table 10. Frequency of PEV Rank for Five Background Factors.

| | Rank | | | | | |
	1	2	3	4	5	Mean
Education	6	3	2	0	1	1.92
Income	2	6	2	2	0	2.33
Age	4	0	4	4	0	2.67
Marital status	0	3	2	4	3	2.75
Race	0	0	2	2	8	4.50

4. It is reasonable that similar scales would be more similar in their background relations than dissimilar scales. To pursue this idea, we set up Table 11; it shows degree of agreement between rank orders of scales within clusters, a cluster being made up of scales with the same simple pattern of factor loadings (see Chapter Three). Scales Nos. 2, 5, 7, 8, and 9 make up Cluster I; Nos. 3, 4, and 6 make up Cluster II. Complete agreement between rank orders requires that no factor appear in more than one column; by inspection it is clear that agreement between ranks within clusters is less than complete.

In Cluster I, education ranks first three times (in five); income ranks second three times; age ranks third three times; marital status and race rank either fourth or fifth four times in five. There is thus only a moderate amount of agreement between ranks in Cluster I. The correlation between ranks as measured by W, the coefficient of concordance, is 0.39 (see Appendix E for formula).

Table 11. Frequency of PEV Rank within Two Clusters.

	Cluster I (2, 5, 7, 8, 9)				
	1	2	3	4	5
Education	3	1	0	0	1
Income	1	3	1	0	0
Age	1	0	3	1	0
Marital status	0	0	1	2	2
Race	0	1	0	2	2

W = 0.39

	Cluster II (3, 4, 6)				
	1	2	3	4	5
Education	1	0	2	0	0
Income	1	1	0	1	0
Age	1	0	0	2	0
Marital Status	0	2	1	0	0
Race	0	0	0	0	3

W = 0.53

In Cluster II, education ranks third two times (in three); age ranks fourth two times; marital status ranks second two times; race ranks fifth three times. However, income fails to occupy the same rank twice. Agreement between ranks within Cluster II is thus far from complete (W = 0.53).

The results of this analysis offer little or no support for the starting proposition that scales similar in content will be similar in their background relations. W (0.44) for both clusters combined was larger than W for Cluster I, smaller than W for Cluster II. These comparisons justify the conclusion that agreement between ranks within clusters is neither better nor worse than agreement of ranks across clusters.

The foregoing analysis (Table 11) has obvious limitations, here briefly noted: (1) The comparison of PEVs within clusters is on the basis of ranks rather than magnitudes. Two or more PEVs may differ in their magnitudes but not in their ranks. For example, Nos. 8 and 9 (Cluster I) differ in their income PEVs, 0.070 to 0.034, yet income has the same rank for both scales. (2) Chance agreement between ranks depends on the number of ranks; for example, five ranks are more likely to agree by chance than ten ranks. We would have had more confidence in our results if scales had had, for instance, ten PEVs instead of five. (3) Chance agreement between rank orders depends on the number of rank orders; for example, two rank orders are more likely to agree by chance than three. We would have more confidence in our results if our clusters had consisted of a dozen or so scales, say, instead of only a handful. Because of these considerations, our results at best have only suggestive value for answering the question whether scales that are similar in content are similar in background relations.

Discussion

Possible Design Effects. In most cases, there was no more than a weak relation between SLFS scores and social background. That was the general rule. We might have come to a different generalization if we had used a different set of operations. We mention here several possibilities:

1. We might have obtained stronger relations, on the average, if we had used a different set of background factors. It is possible that

the social circumstances most strongly related to SLFS scores are only weakly correlated with age, race, education, income, and marital status and that we would have obtained stronger relations between background factors and SLFS scores if we had analyzed factors that were strongly correlated with those particular circumstances. For example, if social life feelings depend most heavily on primary-group relations (weak or strong) or on change in those relations (from better to worse or vice versa), then a grouping of respondents by a measure of primary relations might be expected to show a strong correlation with SLFS scores. We do not know this to be the case; it is a mere possibility.

2. We would have obtained stronger numerical relations if we had based our analysis on finer social classifications, since the finer the classification, the larger the correlation ratio, other things equal. For example, by splitting one or more of the four age groupings (Table 9), we would have obtained larger PEVs for age; likewise, by subdividing one or the other of the race classes, or both, we would have obtained higher coefficients for race. However, it is doubtful that such manipulations would have changed the standing of the explained variance relative to unexplained—it still would have been smaller. In saying this, we assume that the means of smaller classes within larger would differ very little among themselves and for that reason would leave the explained variance largely unchanged. But this is a guess.

3. We might have obtained stronger numerical results if we had transformed SLFS scores before analyzing them. This is not the place to discuss technicalities; suffice it to say, by reducing the skew of scores within classes, we might have raised the standing of the explained variance relative to the unexplained. However, it is quite possible that SLFSs would differ in their reaction to a given transformation. For example, the PEV between feeling down (SLFS3) and income might go up after taking logs, while the PEV between feeling up (SLFS6) and income might go down. And in general the net effect of transforming SLFS scores might be nil. My best guess is that differences among individuals within classes after transforming would continue to overshadow differences of mean scores between classes.

4. We might have obtained larger numerical coefficients if we had given the respondents more latitude in responding to items;

for example, if they had been given four options—strongly agree, agree, disagree, strongly disagree—instead of just two, agree and disagree. In that case, continuing the example, responses would have been scored 0, 1, 2, 3 instead of 0, 1; and that refined scoring might have yielded stronger relations between SLFS scores and background factors. However, this line of reasoning can be extended almost indefinitely. If we had used paired comparisons, or Stevens's psychophysical methods, or Muthén's method, or multidimensional scaling, we would have obtained a different pattern of relations between SLFS scores and background factors. Perhaps all this is merely a reminder that our SLFS scores are method-specific and all that that implies.

   5. It is possible that findings on the relation of SLFS scores were affected by the absence of nonrespondents (see Appendix C). The magnitude and direction of that effect will depend on the similarity of respondents and nonrespondents in their score distributions and in their PEVs. Since that similarity is unknown in the nature of the case, it is possible only to make projections on the basis of this or that assumption. For example, on the assumption of no difference in PEVs on a given factor (for example, age) and no overlap between score distributions on a given scale (for example, No., 2, "Doubt About Trustworthiness of People"), the PEV for respondents and nonrespondents combined would be smaller than for either group separately. Adding nonrespondents to respondents would cause the unexplained variance to increase at the expense of the explained (social background variance) and thereby cause the PEV to become smaller. In this scenario, calculations based on respondents (or nonrespondents) alone would overstate the relation between social background and SLFS scores. We are not suggesting that this is the case; it is one of many possibilities. We draw on it mainly to indicate how the absence of nonrespondents could have affected findings on the relation of social background and SLFS scores. Their absence could have affected other of our findings as well.

   Concluding Remark. Numerous empirical findings lend support to the idea that social life feelings are contingent on social background and vice versa. Opinions and sentiments about society and self are frequently associated with socioeconomic status. Andrews and Withey (1976) found that respondents of low socioeconomic status "tended to be more dissatisfied than others with job pay, family income, financial security, and their standard of living. They felt deprived in meeting their physical needs and they were not as satisfied as others with their health. They had less fun and enjoyment in life and they were discouraged about the prospects of achieving more, getting a better job, etc." (p. 304).

Our findings were generally in line with the idea that differences in social status (broadly defined) are correlated with differences in feelings about self and society. It is almost a tautology that one's view of the social world (as possibly heaven or hell) will depend on one's location in that world. But that view is apparently influenced by other causes as well. We found that differences between classes on such factors as age and education generally carried far less weight than differences among individuals within classes. Our findings thus suggest that we have to go beyond such classifications as age and education to account more completely for individual differences in SLFS scores. That search could lead us to the minutiae of everyday social life, or it could take us to fixed tendencies in the person—personality traits, response sets, and so on. At any rate, we have to acknowledge the limited dependence of SLFS scores on classifications such as income and marital status.

One final point: Our findings demonstrate the necessity of norming score averages on age, race, income, education, and marital status in comparing two or more populations. We have not calculated such normed averages because of uncertainties over the composition of a standard population, but some such standardization would be essential in any comparative study.

6

Relation of Scores to the Ways People Respond to Questions

On questionnaires and in opinion polls, some persons almost always give the socially desirable answer, regardless of their true feelings, while others, in an analogous manner, almost always answer in the affirmative ("agree," "yes," and the like), regardless of their true feelings. Such tendencies have come to be known as response tendencies, or response sets.

The influence of response sets on personality test scores has been a specialty in psychology for over fifty years, and there is a substantial literature on the subject (Edwards, 1957; Block, 1965, Messick, 1968). In the context of the present study, the general idea is that responses to social life feeling items, and composites based on them, are affected by response tendencies as well as by actual social life feelings. These tendencies are stronger in some persons than in others (it is assumed) and are more manifest in some items than in others. Although these ideas are a priori quite plausible, they are extremely difficult to quantify. In any given response, it is very difficult to calculate the weight of a response tendency relative to the weight of the feeling being measured.

However, we felt it important to try, on the assumption that responses to social life feeling items, owing to their relative instability, might be even more subject to the effects of response tendencies than, say, responses to personality items. Accordingly, we undertook to construct a measure of tendency to respond desirably from the 237 social life feeling items on the survey questionnaire, and from the same items a measure of acquiescing. We supposed that such measures might be used to adjust SLFS scores for the effects of responding desirably and acquiescing, respectively. Anticipating the question of how our own response-set scales would compare with previously constructed scales, we included ten items from each of the following scales on the survey questionnaire: Jackson's Social Desirability Scale (1967), Jackson and Messick's Acquiescing Scale (1961), and Marlowe and Crowne's Social Desirability Scale (1960).

First in this chapter, after a few conceptual preliminaries, we give the items in each of the above-mentioned scales and their score characteristics. Second, we discuss the construction of our own scales in some detail and also, but in considerably less detail, the makeup of the three "short forms." Third, we discuss differences in the alpha reliabilities of all five scales and some possible causes of those differences. Fourth, to interpret our own scales, we consider their relation to the three previously constructed scales and to classifications of respondents by age, sex, race, income, education, and marital status. Fifth, we consider the correlations between response-tendency scales and the twelve social life feeling scales. Sixth, we discuss some of the uses of our own measure of responding desirably. And, lastly, we evaluate both that measure and our measure of acquiescing on dimensionality, reliability, and validity.

Conceptual Preliminaries

Most persons now and then, but still infrequently, say they agree with a questionnaire statement when they actually disagree or say they disagree when they actually agree. On the whole, their feelings are accurately represented by their responses. Yet, there are those persons, probably few in number, who frequently say they agree when they actually disagree; similarly, there are those who with some regularity say they disagree when they actually agree. Their feelings are inaccurately represented by their responses.

An acquiescing scale, as it has come to be known, seeks to differentiate between persons given to overagreeing, persons given to underagreeing, and persons given to neither tendency to any marked degree. Persons given to overagreeing will occupy one end of that scale, persons given to underagreeing will occupy the other end, and persons given to neither tendency will be located on the interval between these extreme groups. If the scale has validity, it may be used to adjust content scores by regression for the effect of overagreeing and underagreeing.

Many social life feelings and attitudes are neutral from the standpoint of social desirability. There are some feelings, however, that are generally considered socially desirable and others that are considered undesirable. The feeling that "people should work together for the common good" is generally viewed as desirable, while the feeling that "it is all right to cut throats to get ahead" is regarded as socially undesirable.

As with acquiescing, most persons now and then say they agree with a socially desirable statement when they actually disagree and say they disagree with a socially undesirable statement when they agree. In spite of these discrepancies, observed responses provide an accurate basis for predicting true feelings. But there are those few who, with some regularity, will agree with a socially desirable statement when they actually disagree. We say these persons are given to responding desirably. There are also persons given to responding undesirably—agreeing with socially undesirable statements when they actually disagree and disagreeing with socially desirable statements when they actually agree. For persons with these tendencies, observed responses do not furnish an accurate base for predicting true feelings.

A responding desirably (RD) scale seeks to discriminate between those given to responding desirably, those given to responding undesirably, and those given to neither tendency. On such a scale, persons given to responding desirably stand at one end, persons with the opposite tendency stand at the other, and persons given to neither occupy the middle. Such a scale, if valid, may be used to adjust content scores by regression for the effects of tendency to respond desirably, without regard to one's true feelings.

Scale Contents and Characteristics

We supposed that the average reader would want to familiarize himself or herself with the contents of the scales under study before considering the details of their construction and findings based on their application. Accordingly, at this juncture, for each of five scales—Responding Desirably 16 (RD16), Acquiescing 16 (A16), Jackson Responding Desirably 10 (JRD10), Jackson-Messick Acquiescing 10 (JMA10), and Marlowe-Crowne Social Desirability 10 (MCSD10)— we give individual items and state what scores based on items purport to measure. In addition, for each item we give the keyed response, the percentage giving the keyed response in the national sample, the item-total score correlation, and the first-factor loading (second in the case of A16).

RD16. Responding desirably is the tendency to agree with a socially desirable (SD) statement and to disagree with a socially undesirable (SU) one. RD16 is a measure of that tendency. It consists of sixteen items—eight considered to be SD and eight SU. SD statements are keyed "agree," and SU statements are keyed "disagree." These sixteen items had a mean SD scale value of 6.60 (SD scale values smaller than 5.00 reflected).

Scores of 0 and 16 correspond to no keyed answers and all keyed answers, respectively. In the national sample, scores ranged from a low of 2 to a high of 16—no one made either the lowest possible or the next-lowest possible score. The mean score in the national sample was 12.68; the standard deviation was 2.44. The mean interitem correlation was 0.10; alpha reliability was 0.64.

Responding Desirably (RD16).

Tape No.	Statement	Keyed Response	% Keyed Response	Item-Total Correlation	Factor Loading	SDSV
203	I find that I can help others in many ways.	A	90	.17	.22	7.27
143	I feel that I am better off than my parents were at my age.	A	86	.15	.19	7.26
109	In spite of many changes, there are still definite rules to live by.	A	96	.15	.18	7.18
162	One can always find friends if he tries.	A	92	.22	.27	7.16
75	Anyone can raise his standard of living if he is willing to work at it.	A	89	.14	.17	7.12
181	Most people really believe that honesty is the best policy.	A	77	.29	.34	6.62
118	In general, I am satisfied with my lot in life.	A	83	.29	.36	6.55
19	People will be honest with you as long as you are honest with them.	A	79	.27	.32	6.39
101	It is difficult to think clearly about right and wrong these days.	D	62	.31	.39	4.21
175	Many people are friendly only because they want something from you.	D	53	.29	.37	4.11
64	If the odds are against you, it's impossible to come out on top.	D	66	.24	.32	4.04
155	At times I feel that I am a stranger to myself.	D	79	.24	.31	3.84
128	The future looks very bleak.	D	54	.37	.47	3.77
193	I often feel that no one needs me.	D	81	.29	.37	3.49
114	I am so "fed up" that I can't take it any more.	D	93	.33	.42	3.38
9	To get along with people one must put on an act.	D	87	.33	.41	3.14

Mean SDSV = 6.60

A16. Acquiescing is the tendency to agree (or disagree) with a statement regardless of its content. A16 intends to yield a measure of that tendency. It consists of nine positive statements and seven negative statements, all keyed "agree." (The larger number of positive statements is explained later in the chapter). These sixteen items had a mean SD value of 5.33 (SD scale values smaller than 5.00 reflected). Uniformity in verbal responding is the mark of acquiescing; always choosing the socially desirable response is the mark of responding desirably.

Scores of 0 and 16 correspond to no keyed answers and all keyed answers, respectively. In our sample, approximately 96 percent of all scores fell on the interval 4 to 12; in other words, relatively few scores were below 4 (1.3 percent) or above 12 (2.3 percent), as if few respondents were given to overagreeing or underagreeing. The mean score was 7.86 (0.49 per item); the standard deviation was 2.15. The mean interitem correlation was 0.03, and alpha reliability was 0.37.

Acquiescing (A16).

Tape No.	Statement	Keyed Response	% Keyed Response	Item-Total Correlation[a]	Factor Loading
41	We are slowly losing our freedom to the government.	A	65	.13	.34
49	The government is trying to do too many things.	A	68	.14	.15
63	People are poor because of circumstances beyond their control.	A	57	.06	.04
93	Everything is very uncertain these days.	A	72	.12	.23
130	Prices will keep going up for some time.	A	94	.04	.15
131	This country is in for some hard times.	A	90	.02	.34
209	The federal government is too big.	A	57	.07	.19
51	Our lives are controlled very little by the government.	A	24	-.10	.32
73	Individuals are poor because of the lack of effort on their part.	A	53	-.06	.13
139	In my opinion, poverty will eventually be eliminated in this country.	A	20	-.20	.30
141	In my opinion, the country is heading for prosperity.	A	25	-.08	.43
146	People have more peace of mind today than ever before.	A	14	-.15	.35
147	People live under much less stress today than formerly.	A	23	-.18	.21
179	Few people would use someone else just to get what they want.	A	61	-.19	.20
182	Most people would rather give up their ambition than give up their friends.	A	34	-.12	.15
214	The police treat everyone the same way, regardless of wealth and influence.	A	28	-.09	.24

[a]Items keyed for content.

JRD10. JRD10 consists of ten items from Jackson's twenty-item scale for measuring tendency to respond desirably. The five SD items are keyed "true"; the five SU items are keyed "false." Persons scoring low reject socially desirable statements and accept undesirable ones; persons scoring high reverse this pattern of responding.

Respondents in our sample gave the socially desirable answer approximately eight times in ten. (RD16 and JRD10 are exactly alike in this respect.) Almost 50 percent had scores of 9 or 10, and fewer than 10 percent had scores below 7. This tendency toward high scoring (giving the socially desirable response) is reflected in the median of 8.38. The mean score was 7.92, and the standard deviation was 1.93. The mean interitem correlation was 0.15, and alpha reliability was 0.63.

Jackson Responding Desirably (JRD10).

Tape No.	Statement	Keyed Response[a]	% Keyed Response	Item-Total Correlation	Factor Loading
L1	I find it very difficult to concentrate.	F	75	.38	.52
L2	Rarely, if ever, has the sight of food made me ill.	T	74	.15	.18
L3	Most of my teachers were helpful.	T	87	.17	.20
L4	I often have the feeling that I am doing something evil.	F	90	.29	.37
L5	Many things make me feel uneasy.	F	65	.41	.54
L6	My life is full of interesting activities.	F	73	.35	.43
L7	I am seldom ill.	T	80	.31	.36
L8	I am able to make correct decisions on difficult questions.	T	80	.29	.36
L9	I almost always feel sleepy and lazy.	F	86	.29	.37
L10	I often question whether life is worthwhile.	F	82	.37	.49

[a]F = False, T = True.

JMA10. JMA10 consists of ten items from Jackson and Messick's sixty-item scale for measuring acquiescing. For purposes of scoring, all items are keyed "true." Unlike JRD10, which consists of SD and SU statements in equal numbers, JMA10 consists solely of items considered neutral in social desirability.

Scores in the national sample ranged from 0 to 10 around a mean of 5.92; about six times in ten respondents chose "true" rather than "false." The median of 6.05 was slightly larger than the mean, and the standard deviation of 2.08 was about one third the size of the mean. The mean interitem correlation was 0.11; the corresponding alpha reliability was 0.55.

Jackson-Messick Acquiescing (JMA10).

Tape No.	Statement	Keyed Response	% Keyed Response	Item-Total Correlation	Factor Loading
L11	At times I feel like swearing.	T	70	.16	.16
L12	People have often misunderstood my intentions when I was trying to put them right and be helpful.	T	55	.41	.61
L13	I am apt to hide my feelings in some things to the point that people may hurt me without their knowing about it.	T	65	.29	.41
L14	I like to know some important people because it makes me feel important.	T	29	.22	.27
L15	I have often felt badly over being misunderstood when trying to keep someone from making a mistake.	T	64	.38	.57
L16	I think a great many people exaggerate their misfortunes in order to gain the sympathy and help of others.	T	75	.31	.43
L17	I enjoy detective or mystery stories.	T	61	.03	.02
L18	I wish I could be as happy as others seem to be.	T	34	.26	.35
L19	People generally demand more respect for their own rights than they are willing to allow for others.	T	80	.25	.34
L20	I often must sleep over a matter before I decide what to do.	T	58	.13	.17

MCSD10. MCSD10 consists of ten items from Marlowe and Crowne's scale for measuring social desirability (SD). Five items are socially desirable and five socially undesirable. Persons scoring high mark SD statements true and SU statements false. Low scorers reverse this pattern of responding.

Scores in the national sample ranged from 0 to 10, although fewer than 5 percent scored below 3. Respondents considered SD statements to be true and SU statements to be false approximately two times in three. On the average, respondents tended to present themselves in a favorable light. The mean score in the national sample was 6.42; the standard deviation was 2.45. The mean interitem correlation was 0.20; alpha reliability was 0.72.

Marlowe-Crowne Social Desirability (MCSD10).

Tape No.	Statement	Keyed Response	% Keyed Response	Item-Total Correlation	Factor Loading
L21	There have been times when I was quite jealous of the good fortune of others.	F	66	.40	.48
L22	No matter who I'm talking to, I'm always a good listener.	T	76	.38	.45
L23	I never resent being asked to return a favor.	T	85	.25	.30
L24	I sometimes try to get even rather than forgive and forget.	F	74	.42	.51
L25	I sometimes feel resentful when I don't get my way.	F	57	.45	.55
L26	I have never deliberately said something that hurt someone's feelings.	T	55	.36	.42
L27	There have been occasions when I felt like smashing things.	F	37	.32	.39
L28	I have never intensely disliked anyone.	T	53	.34	.40
L29	There have been occasions when I took advantage of someone.	F	62	.44	.54
L30	I'm always willing to admit it when I make a mistake.	T	77	.40	.47

Constructing Scales

JMA10 and JRD10. Jackson and Messick (1961) reasoned that responses to statements diverse in content and neutral in social desirability would reflect acquiescing and that responses to statements diverse in content and extreme in social desirability would reflect tendency to respond desirably. To investigate these possibilities, they arrayed 290 Minnesota Multiphasic Personality Test items by degree of social desirability and took scores based on sixty items in the middle of the distribution as a measure of acquiescing, and scores based on the fifty most desirable items at one end and the 60 least desirable at the other as measures of responding desirably.

Later Jackson combined splits of the twenty best items from each of the aforesaid end groupings of fifty and sixty items and took scores based on these forms as measures of responding desirably. In other words, he set up two forms, each consisting of ten socially desirable and ten socially undesirable statements. These two forms, denoted AA and BB, appear in his Personality Research Form (1967).

In constructing a short form of Jackson's social desirability scale (Form AA), hereafter denoted JRD10 (*RD* stands for responding desirably, and *10* stands for ten items), we took into account both the correlations of items with total score and the classification of items as socially desirable or socially undesirable. From the ten items considered socially desirable, we chose the five with the highest correlations with scores based on all twenty; and from the ten items considered socially undesirable, we similarly chose the five with the highest total-score correlations. We supposed that a combination selected in this manner would be more predictive of total score than alternative combinations of ten.

In constructing a short form of Jackson and Messick's acquiescing scale, denoted JMA10 (*A* stands for acquiescing), we took into account both the correlations of items with scores based on all sixty items and their location in the interval considered neutral in social desirability. From the lower half of the neutral interval, we chose the five items with the highest correlations with total score; and from the upper half, we similarly chose the five items with the highest correlations. Here, as in the case of JRD10, we supposed that a combination selected in this way would be more predictive of total score than alternative combinations.

Constructing RD16. In constructing a measure of responding desirably from the 237 SLF items on the survey questionnaire, we sought items diverse in content and high or low in social desirability, in the manner of Jackson and Messick. Such a combination of items might be expected to serve as a measure of responding desirably by this reasoning: few persons are uniformly high or uniformly low in all their social life feelings; however, some persons respond to questionnaire items as if they were. Since such uniformity cannot be plausibly ascribed to social life feelings, it must be due to tendency to respond desirably. By this argument, a list of items spread evenly across diverse content areas and balanced on social desirability within content areas might be expected to serve as an index of tendency to respond desirably.

In compiling such a list, we had, first, to scale items by degree of social desirability and, second, to select pairs of socially desirable and undesirable items from a wide range of content areas, or topics. Here are the details.

Item scaling: For a first round of SD scale values (SDSVs), we turned to college students—750 in all. These 750 students from fifteen classes supplied 250 ratings for each of 270 items, with no student rating more than ninety items or so. Students were instructed to rate the social desirability of "a number of statements that people make about themselves, about others, and about life in general" (for example, "Anyone can raise his standard of living if he is willing to work at it"), quite apart from their own agreement with the content of those statements. For scaling items, a 9-point rating scale was provided, with "most desirable" at one end represented by 9, "least desirable" at the other end represented by 1, and "neutral" in the middle represented by 5. Not unexpectedly, subjects differed widely among themselves on the scale location of some items and differed very little on the location of others. Of the unambiguous items, some were near the neutral value of 5, while a substantial number were some distance away. This latter group of items would be suitable for measuring tendency to respond desirably among college students.

To identify items suitable for measuring responding desirably in the general (adult) population, we turned to a random sample of 295 adults resident in Indianapolis, Indiana. (For sampling details, see Schuessler, Hittle, and Cardascia, 1978.) This field survey yielded SDSVs for 195 items (selected from those previously administered to college students), each SDSV based on 295 ratings.

The Indianapolis ratings were similar in the pattern of their distribution to the college student ratings. They differed in two main respects: (1) ratings for individual items were more widely dispersed around their mean value, and (2) mean values (SDSVs) were less widely scattered over their range. Indianapolis respondents, to a greater degree than college students, tended to avoid the extreme categories; they differed more among themselves on the location of items on the scale. This finding suggested that SDSVs might be correlated to some degree with social background.

For evidence on this point (see Dohrenwend and Dohrenwend, 1969) we compared SDSV distributions for men and women, whites and nonwhites, high school graduates and nongraduates, and persons over forty-five years of age (old) and persons under forty-five years (young). We found little or no difference between men and women; little or no difference between old and young; some difference between graduates and nongraduates; and a substantial difference between whites and nonwhites.

For additional evidence, we set up SDSV distributions for race-by-education subgroups and compared each of these four subgroups with every other for a total of six comparisons. These comparisons pointed to a probable race-by-education interaction in the variation of individual ratings on some of the items. In view of this likelihood, we decided to subject every item otherwise eligible for membership in the responding desirably scale to a race-by-education analysis of variance with the idea of screening out every item with a significant (0.05) interaction and with cell means arrayed around the neutral value of 5.00.

Item selection. Items were selected so that as a group they would express a wide variety of social life feelings and divide equally between socially desirable and socially undesirable statements. In choosing items, our starting pool consisted of the 195 items judged by the Indianapolis sample. From this set of 195, we first discarded every item whose standard deviation (for individual ratings) was larger than the median of all 195 standard deviations and whose

SDSV fell within the interquartile range of the 195 SDSVs. This screening left us with seventy-seven items whose individual ratings were relatively homogeneous and whose SDSVs were relatively high or low.

Second, from this group of seventy-seven, we dropped all items with a significant race-by-education interaction and with cell means arrayed around the neutral value of 5.00. This screening left us with fifty-five items whose individual ratings were relatively homogeneous and whose SDSVs were uniformly low or high across race-by-education subgroups.

Third, we cross-classified items by key (agree = socially desirable, disagree = socially undesirable) and by fourteen content categories (see Appendix B), with the idea of selecting one pair of differently keyed items from each of the fourteen content areas. On cross-classifying we discovered that only eight of the fourteen categories were represented by at least one pair and that we would therefore be limited to eight pairs—six short of our quota. Choosing the best pair (where choice was possible) from each of eight categories gave us sixteen items heterogeneous in content and either high or low in social desirability. These sixteen items, already given, make up RD16.

Constructing A16. In constructing a measure of acquiescing (overagreeing and underagreeing) we assumed, again following Jackson and Messick, that the weight of this tendency in a given response is affected by both the content of an item and its social desirability and that both must be taken into account in selecting items for such a measure. That is the sense of the requirement that items for measuring acquiescing be neutral in social desirability and representative of diverse content areas.

To control for social desirability, we restricted eligibility to items with social desirability scale values (SDSVs) between 4.5 and 5.5 and with standard deviations smaller than the median. To control for content, we planned to draw one item from each of two keys (agree and disagree) within fourteen different topics, or content areas. However, we had to give up that plan because not every topic within each key had at least one item. As an alternative, we picked ten items that were weakly correlated among themselves from each key (agree and disagree), for a total of twenty. The rationale of this procedure was that only those persons given to overagreeing (under-agreeing) would agree (disagree) to all twenty such statements, or practically all, since most persons in the sample tended to shift back and forth between agree and disagree, as indicated by the weak correlations between items both within and across keys.

After much trial and error—we considered at least ten possibilities—we settled on a combination of seven agree-keyed (for content) items and nine disagree-keyed (for content) items. (Scores based on these sixteen were almost perfectly correlated with scores based on all twenty.) These sixteen items make up A16 (*16* stands for 16 items), with all items keyed "agree."

With this uniform keying (that is, all items keyed "agree"), the mean interitem correlation is 0.03, and the mean item-total correlation (signs disregarded) is 0.10. Corresponding figures for the same items keyed for content are 0.06 and 0.17, respectively. This contrast shows that in rekeying items for acquiescing we weakened the relation of items to total score and thereby lowered the alpha reliability of that score. It points generally to the problem of getting a reliable measure of acquiescing from a set of key-balanced items whose correlations are all positive when keyed for content. We come back to this point in comparing the reliabilities of all five response-set scores.

MCSD10. Marlowe and Crowne (1960) sought to measure that part of responding desirably that is attributable to an individual's need for social approval. The main idea is that a need for social approval expresses itself in responding desirably and that responding desirably is therefore indicative of need for social approval. Their test consists of eighteen socially desirable statements keyed "true" and fifteen socially undesirable statements keyed "false." The socially desirable items refer to good behaviors that few people display all the time, and the socially undesirable items refer to bad behaviors that most people display some of the time. For example, few people are good listeners all the time (a socially desirable trait), and most people are jealous of the good luck of others (an undesirable reaction) some of the time. Persons given to responding desirably and presumably in need of social approval claim that all their reactions are good and none are bad. For example, I am always a good listener; I am never jealous of the good luck of others.

In selecting items from Marlowe and Crowne's list of thirty-three, we gave equal representation to keys, and within keys we selected items most predictive of total score. From the eighteen socially desirable statements, we selected the five with the highest correlations with scores based on all thirty-three; and from the fifteen socially undesirable statements, we chose the five items with the highest correlations with total score. MCSD10 is the outcome of that selection process. As with JRD10 and JMA10, we assumed that a combination made up in this way would be more predictive of total score than alternative combinations of ten items. (For a reinterpretation of the Marlowe = Crowne scale, see Bradburn and Sudman, 1979.)

Reliability

Of the three ten-item response-set scales, MCSD10 had the highest reliability (0.72) and JMA10, the lowest (0.55). Of the two sixteen-item scales, RD16 had the higher reliability.

To draw comparisons among the reliabilities of all five scales, we gave to each of the ten-item scales the statistical advantage of six additional items. This adjustment put both JMA10 and JRD10 above RD16 but (of course) did not change their standing relative to MCSD10 or to each other. Table 12 provides the numerical detail:

Since alpha reliability is a function of the mean correlation between items, differences in reliability are directly attributable to differences in mean correlation and indirectly to whatever produced

Table 12. Reliability of Response Set Measures.

| | Alpha reliability | |
Scale	Unadjusted	Adjusted
RD16	0.64	0.64
A16	0.37	0.37
JMA10	0.55	0.66
JRD10	0.63	0.73
MCSD10	0.72	0.80

those differences. Differences in mean correlation could be due at least in part to differences between personality items and social life feeling items in subject (grammatical). Personality items usually have the personal pronoun *I* as subject, whereas social life feeling items have diverse subjects—*it, they, people, world*. Responses to impersonal statements about the world or people in general are probably more subject to random disturbances than personal statements about self, and correlations between them might therefore be expected to be lower. The lower reliabilities of RD16 and A16 relative to JRD10, JMA10, and MCSD10 could be accounted for by this line of reasoning.

Differences in mean correlation (or reliability) could also be due to systematic differences between responses to items neutral in SD and responses to items high or low in SD. Responses to items high or low in SD are probably less subject to random disturbances, and their correlations might accordingly be expected to be higher than correlations between items neutral in SD. This factor could account for the higher reliability of RD16 relative to A16 and the higher reliability of MCSD10 and JRD10 relative to JMA10.

If our lines of reasoning are correct, we would expect scores based on SD or SU statements with *I* as subject to have higher reliabilities than scores based on neutral (in SD) items with a noun as subject, other things equal.

Validity

Interscale Correlations. It is a truism that a scale is valid if it measures what it purports to measure. With scales such as RD16 and A16 it is practically impossible to measure their validity directly; it is possible only to judge their validity from their relation to seemingly relevant variables. For judging the validity of RD16 and A16, we examined their relation to JRD10, JMA10, and MCSD10; their relation to selected classifications; and the relation of RD16 to item SDSVs. (We note in passing that today the subject of validity is very much on the minds of specialists on mental testing, because of the criticism that many of their tests do an injustice to racial and ethnic minorities; see Messick, 1979.)

We consider first the relation of RD16 and A16, respectively, to JRD10, JMA10, and MCSD10 (Table 13). RD16 had its largest correlation with JRD10 and its smallest with MCSD10. These correlations suggest that RD16 and JRD10 may be measuring the same trait but that RD16 and MCSD10 are probably measuring different traits. RD16's correlation with JRD10 is evidence for its validity as a measure of responding desirably, assuming that JRD10 is itself a valid measure of that tendency. It does not demonstrate validity in the sense of capacity to discriminate between known groups, because Jackson's test was not validated by that method. It is a finding for concurrent validity in the sense of estimating scores based on a different test of the same trait administered to the same persons at the same time. (According to *Standards for Educational and Psychological Tests* [American Psychological Association, 1974], "Statements of concurrent validity indicate the extent to which the test may be used to estimate an individual's present standing on the criterion.")

Table 13. Correlations Between Response Set Measures.

	A16	JRD10	JMA10	MCSD10
RD16	-0.22	0.54	-0.36	0.16
A16		-0.26	0.17	0.15
JRD10			-0.36	0.19
JMA10				-0.24

The correlations for A16 give practically no support to its validity as a measure of acquiescing. Contrary to expectation, A16 had a stronger correlation (although negative) with JRD10 than with JMA10. This finding is no less damaging to the validity of JMA10 as a measure of acquiescing than it is to the validity of A16; it may be that both scales are lacking in validity or that acquiescing is specific to content.

The negative correlation between RD16 and A16 (-.022) is subject to at least two interpretations: first, it may be a mere consequence of reflecting variables or rekeying items. The complete (100 percent) unbalancing of one of two key-balanced scales whose correlation is positive will yield a smaller and possibly negative correlation between the key-balanced and key-uniform scale. Since the correlation between RD16 and A16 with all items keyed for content was positive (0.17), it was a foregone conclusion that the correlation between RD16 and A16 (all items keyed "agree") would be smaller and possibly negative. Second, the same factor causing responding desirably to increase in the person may cause acquiescing to decrease, and vice versa. In this view the negative correlation between RD16 and A16 is attributable to social circumstances that influence both response tendencies but in different ways. We develop this point in discussing the relation of RD16 and A16 to social background.

Response-Set Measures and Social Background. Since social behavior is influenced by social background, and since response tendencies are social behavior, we assumed that RD16 and A16 scores would differ by categories of social background—age, sex, and so on. The absence of any such differences would be against their validity, whereas the presence of differences would be for their possible validity but not proof of it. Our exploration of the relation of RD16 and A16 to various social classifications was based on this supposition. We also supposed that our findings would be suggestive of the manner in which social background influences biased responding.

Table 14 gives mean scores for categories within six social classifications. It may be viewed as a device for predicting categories from scores or the reverse—for predicting scores from categories. We consider first the efficiency of scales for predicting background categories and then the efficiency of categories for predicting individual response-set scores. Lastly, we consider the similarity of response-set scales in ranking categories within social classifications.

Predicting categories: Table 14 shows that RD16 does best (PEV = 0.09) in predicting income and next best in predicting years of schooling; it has no value for predicting sex and practically none for predicting age, race, or marital status. A16 does best in predicting education (PEV = 0.11); it does relatively well in predicting age and income; like RD16, it has only negligible value for classifying respondents by sex, race, and marital status.

Table 14. Mean Scores for RD16, A16, JRD10, JMA10, and MCSD10 by Selected Social Classifications.

Classification	RD16	JRD10	MCSD10	A16	JMA10
Age					
18–29	12.23	7.66	5.46	7.38	6.09
30–44	12.92	8.20	6.14	7.54	5.92
45–59	12.92	8.14	6.98	8.02	5.90
60+	12.45	7.40	7.56	9.02	5.72
PEV[a]	.016	.026	.092	.064	.003
Sex					
Men	12.71	8.12	6.22	7.93	6.07
Women	12.66	7.80	6.56	7.81	5.81
PEV	.000	.007	.005	.001	.004
Race					
White	12.84	8.04	6.35	7.75	5.77
Black	11.75	7.30	6.84	8.49	6.82
PEV	.025	.018	.005	.015	.032
Family income					
Under $8,000	11.80	7.31	6.67	8.53	6.32
$8,000–12,000	12.85	7.92	6.57	7.72	5.94
Over $12,000	13.46	8.58	5.95	7.33	5.54
PEV	.093	.085	.018	.062	.027
Education					
Less than 12 years	11.94	7.18	6.99	8.74	6.34
12 years	12.96	8.17	6.58	7.64	5.70
More than 12 years	13.29	8.56	5.60	7.02	5.63
PEV	.058	.093	.056	.112	.024
Marital status					
Married	12.97	8.12	6.43	7.78	5.80
Widowed	12.17	7.51	7.36	8.42	5.75
Divorced	12.04	7.45	6.47	7.98	6.49
Single	12.20	7.68	5.44	7.65	6.20
PEV	.027	.021	.038	.011	.013

[a]Percentage explained variance.

JRD10 does best in predicting education and next best in predicting income; it has no value for grouping respondents by sex and only slight value for grouping them by age, race, and marital status categories. JMA10 (which has the lowest average predictive efficiency) does best with race and next best with income; it does poorly with marital status and even worse with age and sex.

MCSD10 does best in predicting age, next best in predicting years of schooling; it has no value for classifying persons by sex and race and only slight value for income. (It is to be understood that all the above statements apply to relative rather than absolute magnitudes.)

Predicting scores: In predicting scores from categories, we find that age does best with MCSD10 (PEV = 0.09) and next best with A16; it has no value for predicting JMA10 and almost none for predicting RD16 and JRD10. Race does best with JMA10 and next best with RD16; it has no utility for predicting scores on MCSD10.

Income does best with RD16 and next best with JRD10; its efficiency in predicting MCSD10 is negligible. Education does best with A16 and next best with JRD10; it does relatively poorly with JMA10. Marital status resembles race in that none of its explained variances reaches 4 percent; it serves best to predict MCSD10. Sex has predictive utility for none of the five response-set scales.

When we consider scales two or more at a time, we find that RD16 and JRD10 are similar in their rankings of categories by means, and A16, JMA10, and MCSD10 are similar in theirs. Within each of these divisions, rankings are alike on sex, race, income, and education and different on age or marital status or both. Average scores for RD16 and JRD10 were higher for men, whites, higher incomes, and more education; the reverse pattern held for A16, JMA10, and MCSD10. It thus appears that the upper social classes are more given to responding desirably, while the lower social classes are more given to acquiescing (disregarding MCSD10).

We may speculate (see Lenski and Leggett, 1960; Carr, 1971) that the tendency of the upper classes to respond desirably is an affirmation of faith in the American creed, since the main tenets of that creed correspond closely to what is considered socially desirable (individualism, work, integrity, success, and so on). In analogous fashion, the tendency of the lower classes to overagree may be a function of their economic powerlessness and social insecurity ("agree with me or lose your job"). From this point of view, both responding desirably and acquiescing are cultural techniques for getting along in American society: the upper classes find it useful to respond desirably habitually; the lower classes to yea-say (rather than nay-say) habitually.

All such speculations must be taken with critical reserve. Our findings are consistent with the hypothesis (post factum) that socio-economic status is a factor in both responding desirably and yea-saying and possibly is the cause of the negative correlation between them. However, our findings on these group differences serve to validate neither RD16 nor A16, since the observed differences between social and economic categories were based on the very tests whose respective validities were in question.

   RD16-Item Correlations. If items high or low in social desirability are more subject to the influence of responding desirably than neutral items, and if RD16 is a valid measure of responding desirably, then items high or low in SD should show more correlation with RD16 than items neutral in SD.

   In considering this possibility, we first dropped those items—97 of 195—whose standard deviations were larger than the median value, on the assumption that such relatively ambiguous items (items with relatively large standard deviations) would be inconsistently related to RD16. (Since an SDSV is the mean of as many ratings as judges, it necessarily has a standard deviation.) Second, we dropped all items appearing in RD16. This left us with 82 items for doing the analysis.

   To check our starting hunch that RD16's correlations with items high or low in SD would be stronger than its correlations with items neutral in SD, we set up a cross-tabulation of item-RD16 correlations by item SDSVs. This is Table 15. This tabulation shows that no negative correlation was paired with an SDSV larger than 5.0, and no positive correlation was paired with an SDSV smaller than 5.0. From the sign of the correlation, we can predict perfectly whether an item's SDSV will be above or below 5.00.

   For negative correlations larger (numerically) than 0.30, the chances are 100 percent that the SDSV is smaller than 4.5—the lower bound of the neutral interval. For negative correlations larger than 0.20, the chances are about 85 percent that the SDSV is smaller than 4.5. From the magnitude of a negative correlation, we can predict with fair accuracy whether the SDSV will be smaller than 4.5, or below the neutral interval.

   For positive correlations larger than 0.20, the chances are about 85 percent that the SDSV is smaller than 4.5. From the magnitude of a negative correlation, we can predict with 100 percent accuracy that the SDSV will be larger than 5.5, the upper

Table 15. Item-RD16 Correlations (Rows) by Item SDSVs (Columns).

	4.0-4.4	4.5-4.9	5.0-5.4	5.5-5.9	6.0-6.4	6.5-6.9	7.0-7.4
0.50-0.41	2						
0.40-0.31	8						
(-) 0.30-0.21	2	2					
0.20-0.11		3					
0.10-0.01		2					
0							
0.00-0.09			6	1	1	2	
0.10-0.19			5	7	6	3	1
(+) 0.20-0.29				2	13	5	1
0.30-0.39			1	1	4	1	1
0.40-0.49					2		
	12	7	12	11	26	11	3

bound of the neutral interval; for the same grouping, we can predict
with around 90 percent accuracy that the SDSV will be larger than
6.00.

These actuarial predictions are somewhat crude, except that
sign discriminates perfectly between SDSVs above and below 5.0, or
the neutral point. None of these findings is a strict demonstration of
validity; all conform to what one would expect if RD16 were a valid
measure of responding desirably.

Relation of SLFSs to Response-Set Scales

Constructing RD16 and A16 was undertaken in the first place
with the idea of adjusting social life feeling scales for the effects of
responding desirably and acquiescing. Also, at the time, we expected
that the items making up our response-set scales would be drawn
largely, if not wholly, from items appearing in one or more of our
projected content scales. In this we were mistaken; of the ninety-five
different items appearing in the twelve SLFSs, five appeared in
RD16 and two appeared in A16; none appeared in both. Our expectation that many items might do double duty failed to materialize.

The dependence of SLFS scores on response bias may be gauged from the detail of Table 16. It gives the partial variances (as percentages) for the twelve social life feeling scales after adjustment on response-set scales by linear regression. The smaller the partial variance, the larger the adjustment.

Column averages show that response-set scales differed in their average effects; row averages show that SLFSs differed in their average adjustments. MCSD10 had the smallest average effect (mean partial variance = 98) and RD16 the largest; SLFS1 had the largest average adjustment (mean partial variance = 80) and SLFS12 the smallest.

Row differences within columns reflect differences between SLFSs for a given response-set measure. The partial variance of SLFS1 after adjustment on RD16 was 69, a 31 percent reduction in variance, while its partial variance was 100 after adjustment on MCSD10, and 0 percent reduction.

Table 16 suggests that there would be little or no point in adjusting social life feeling scores on MCSD10, since that adjustment has little effect on SLFS variances generally. It also suggests that either RD16 or JRD10, but not necessarily both, might be used

Table 16. Percentage Partial Variances for Twelve SLFSs After Adjustment on Response-Set Scales.

SLFS	RD16	JRD10	MCSD10	A16	JMA10	Mean
1	64	72	99	81	85	80
2	62	90	100	97	90	88
3	72	71	96	98	86	84
4	89	92	97	99	98	95
5	88	96	99	100	99	96
6	70	71	98	98	92	86
7	82	97	97	82	94	89
8	82	92	100	92	95	92
9	69	84	100	92	93	88
10	90	96	95	98	99	96
11	72	66	100	86	92	83
12	100	100	100	97	99	99
Mean	78	93	86	94	98	

to adjust SLFSs for tendency to respond desirably. Although partial variances for RD16 and JRD10 are similar in their rank orders, they differ in their absolute magnitudes, RD16's generally being the smaller.

The case for using either A16 or JMA10 as a control on acquiescing is less compelling. Their partial variances tend to be large, on the average, and the relation of one series to the other as either magnitudes or ranks is quite erratic. A16 shows more partial variances smaller than 90 (3 to 1) and by that criterion might be considered to be the more effective control; however, both are relatively ineffective, and a good case could be made for adjusting SLFSs on neither.

Uses of RD16 and A16

On an abstract level, RD16 and A16 have the same major uses; however, the use of A16 as a research instrument would be difficult to justify because of its low reliability. For that reason, we limit our discussion to RD16. It is understood that before using RD16 (or any such scale) its limitations would have to be taken carefully into account.

RD16 as Control Variable. Constructing RD16 was based on the assumption that SLFS scores might be raised or lowered by the tendency to respond desirably and that such scores should be adjusted for that bias before analyzing them. We wondered whether differences between white and nonwhite SLFS scores, for example, might be caused by differences in responding desirably and whether such differences might vanish after adjusting them for that response bias. This possibility has been considered in previous investigations: Dohrenwend and Dohrenwend (1969); Gove and Geerken (1977); Phillips and Segal (1969).

To exemplify this approach, we give the results of a covariance analysis of two social life feeling scales (Nos. 1 and 6) for four social classifications (age, race, income, and education) with RD16 as the covariate, or control. These results are given in Table 17. In every comparison but one—between races on No. 6—differences between means remained significant after correcting for regression on RD16. Differences between means were generally smaller after adjustment; also, means by age categories changed their rank order on both No. 1 and No. 6. In no case did a difference not significant before adjustment become significant afterward. The lone case of a significant difference losing significance is a reminder that a difference between social categories in SLFS scores may be due to a difference between categories in responding desirably. In this case, after making an allowance for the stronger tendency of whites to respond desirably, the difference in mean scores on SLFS6 lost its significance.

　　RD16 as Dependent Variable. Instead of trying to account for differences in SLFS scores by correcting them for responding desira-

Table 17. Means on SLFS1 and SLFS6 for Four Classifications, Before and After Adjusting on RD16.

		SLFS1		SLFS6	
		Unadjusted	Adjusted	Unadjusted	Adjusted
Classification		Mean	Mean	Mean	Mean
Age[a]					
18–29	(400)	5.21	4.83	3.02	2.77
30–44	(441)	4.95	5.18	2.73	2.88
45–59	(448)	5.99	6.22	2.98	3.13
60+	(225)	7.43	7.24	3.80	3.67
		(s)[b]	(s)	(s)	(s)
Race					
White	(1298)	5.34	5.47	2.91	3.00
Black	(184)	7.79	7.01	3.71	3.18
		(s)	(s)	(s)	(ns)[c]
Education					
Less than 12 years	(549)	7.78	7.21	3.72	3.30
12 years	(495)	5.28	5.48	2.78	2.93
More than 12 years	(463)	3.66	4.12	2.48	2.84
		(s)	(s)	(s)	(s)
Family income					
Under $8,000	(521)	7.27	6.59	3.96	3.48
$8,000–12,000	(300)	5.59	5.59	2.78	2.87
Over $12,000	(522)	4.06	4.67	2.20	2.62
		(s)	(s)	(s)	(s)

[a]Interaction with RD16 significant at 0.05 level.
[b]s = significant at 0.05 level.
[c]ns = not significant at 0.05 level.

bly, we may try to account for differences in tendency to respond desirably by relating them to differences in social and personal factors. In this view, responding desirably is an effect to be explained rather than a disturbance to be controlled. There is an almost endless list of factors that might contribute to differences in tendency to respond desirably. We have stressed such social factors as education and income; psychologists lay greater stress on such factors as need and motivation. Each of these emphases points to a somewhat distinctive line of research. Sociologists are more likely to concentrate on differences between cultural groups in responding desirably, while psychologists are more likely to concentrate on individual differences within such groups. RD16 might find a use in all such studies.

Other Uses. We have expanded on RD16 as control variable, and as dependent variable to a lesser extent, mainly because we had these uses in mind when we constructed it. We did foresee other uses, and we mention some of these in closing this discussion.

1. RD16 might be used as a device for eliminating items markedly subject to responding desirably from content scales. Jackson (1967) used his responding scale for this purpose.

2. RD16 might be used to study the relation of test scores to actual social behavior. A person may score low on RD16 and yet be given to responding desirably in interpersonal relations; or a person may score high on RD16 and yet show no sign of responding desirably in everyday conduct. RD16 could be used in efforts to answer the question whether questionnaire measures of responding desirably are predictive of actual social behavior, and vice versa.

3. It would be possible to stratify a sample by RD16 scores and to compare respondents within and between strata in respect to their SLFS scores. That breakdown would indicate whether respondents with the highest and lowest RD16 scores tend to be uniformly high or low in their SLFS profiles. A finding to the contrary would call into question our assumption that uniformly high or low SLFS profiles are attributable to responding desirably.

4. A stratification of respondents by RD16 would also indicate whether a path model (structural equation model) of the relation of SLFS scores and exogenous variables held equally for respondents with very high RD16 scores, very low, and in between.

A finding to the contrary would raise the question whether respondents with very high (low) RD16 scores should perhaps be dropped from the analysis, much as MMPI test results are sometimes disregarded when K and L scores are improbably high.

Evaluation and Summary

To this point, critical questions about RD16 and A16 have been rasied more or less in passing; they pertain mainly to dimensionality, reliability, validity, and use. Here we summarize our findings on these matters and discuss them as they relate to the adequacy of RD16 and A16 as research instruments.

Dimensionality. We did not specify in advance the dimensionality of RD16 and A16 (as we did with the SLFSs); their dimensionality was free to vary, one might say. However, as it turned out, our method of selecting items in each case worked against unidimensionality and virtually assured multidimensionality.

On factoring RD16's interitem correlations, we obtained four significant factors. Correlating RD16 with factor scores gave a value close to 1.00 for the first factor and values smaller than 0.25 for the other three. The first factor had moderately large loadings in all items (p. 93), while the other three loaded in only two or three items apiece. Our interpretation of this pattern is that the first (general) factor is tendency to respond desirably and that the lesser factors are specific feelings whose effects we had failed to neutralize in our choice of items. This interpretation is consistent with the similarity of content between items loading on the same specific factor: the second factor loads in items expressive of trust (Nos. 181 and 19); the third, items expressive of personal satisfaction (Nos. 203 and 118); the fourth, items indicative of morale (Nos. 155 and 128). These similarities in content, we surmise, account for the presence of specific factors.

Factoring A16's interitem correlations gave five significant factors. Loadings on the first factor were all positive; loadings on the second factor were negative for negatively worded items and positive for positively worded items. A16 had a correlation of 0.26 with the first-factor score and a correlation of 0.74 with the second-factor score; correlations with other factor scores were below 0.25.

Our interpretation of these results is that the first factor is a content factor that tends to raise the correlations between items (keyed for content) and that the second factor is a direction-of-wording, or acquiescing, factor that tends to lower the correlations between items (keyed for content). Although A16 had its largest correlation with the second-factor score, which we took to be a measure of acquiescing, there would be little or no point in replacing A16 by that score, since it is no more reliable than A16 itself.

Reliability. Since alpha reliability decreases as the mean interitem correlation decreases, anything that causes that mean to decrease will necessarily bring about a lowering of alpha reliability.

In the case of RD16, the mean interitem correlation was held down by our method of selecting items. Choosing items that were heterogeneous in content necessarily gave us weakly correlated items and, in consequence, a relatively low alpha reliabilty for total scores. We could have raised reliability by giving up some balance in content (a set of thirteen pairs of differently keyed items with five of eight categories represented by two pairs each had an alpha reliability of 0.75, for example) or by including more socially undesirable statements than socially desirable (interitem correlations between undesirable statements are higher, on the average). However, we decided against those changes in order to maintain as much comparability with JRD10 as possible.

In the case of A16, reliability was held down by choosing weakly correlated items within keys and by keying all items "agree" regardless of their direction. With this keying, the mean interitem correlation was 0.03 and the corresponding alpha reliability 0.37. This finding calls attention to the problem of constructing a reliable measure of tendency to acquiesce from what amounts to a key-balanced content score.

Validity. In studying RD16's validity, we considered its relation to previously constructed SD scales, its correlations with SD and SU items, and its relation to various social classifications.

RD16 had moderately high concurrent validity with JRD10 as the criterion but little or no concurrent validity with MCSD10 as the criterion. It appears that there is little or no connection between whatever is being measured by MCSD10, possibly approval need, and whatever is being measured by RD16, possibly responding desirably.

RD16 discriminated between age, race, income, education, and marital status groupings. However, these differences do not validate RD16; they are merely what one would expect if RD16 were a valid measure of responding desirably.

We reasoned that RD16 would show stronger correlation with items high or low in SD than with neutral items on the assumption that such items would be more subject to the influence of tendency to respond desirably. Although it was not possible to predict accurately an item's SDSV from its correlation with RD16, it was possible to predict with fair accuracy its classification as SD or SU from the sign and magnitude of that correlation.

None of the above findings is against the possibility that RD16 is a valid measure of RD; however, none rules out competing interpretations. First, an RD16 score could be regarded as an index of respondent's social life feeling profile—uniformly high, uniformly low, or in between. From this standpoint, high and low scores on RD16 correspond to those persons who are extreme, in all their social life feelings, at one end or the other. Our interpretation of RD16 as a measure of RD assumes that few if any such persons exist and that indications to the contrary are an effect of responding desirably.

Second, an RD16 score might be interpreted as a reflection of an individual's underlying temperament—happy or sad (suggestion due to Howard Schuman). Happy (sanguine) persons would necessarily score high; sad (melancholy) persons would necessarily score low. Middle scores would signify no marked tendency toward either extreme. This interpretation requires that the ratio of temperamentally happy to sad persons in the population change more or less continuously over time, since RD16 scores differ by social categories, and the distribution of the population by social categories changes over time. A fluctuating ratio of happy to sad persons poses no problem if we regard temperament as a socially conditioned response; it does pose a problem if we regard temperament as genetically determined. The interpretation of responding desirably as a technique of adjusting to specific social circumstances is free of this problem.

We make no strong claim for the validity of A16. Many findings in our research indicate that people differ in their tendency to overagree or underagree and that this tendency is a component in A16. For example, we found that from the sign of the correlation between A16 and a content score (author, topic, subject class, SLFS) it is generally possible to predict whether the majority of items are keyed "agree" or "disagree." The sign is almost always positive when a majority of items are keyed "agree" and negative when the items are keyed "disagree." However, from the magnitude of the correlation it is not possible to predict the ratio of agree- to disagree-keyed items, whether it tends to 1 or 0. We have not given these and related findings in detail, since they have little or no practical value; they are of methodological interest mainly. As noted earlier, our discussion of A16 serves primarily to direct attention to the difficulties of devising a pure measure of acquiescing.

Uses of RD16 and A16. The abstract uses of RD16 and A16 come readily to mind: as measures of disturbances to be controlled and as measures of effects to be explained. However, we do not advise the use of A16, owing to its unsatisfactory reliability, except for purely exploratory purposes. And we suggest that RD16 be used advisedly. RD16 scores should not be uncritically accepted as valid measures of responding desirably, but rather treated tentatively as if they could be valid measures of that tendency.

With this reservation, we foresee that RD16, or a refined version, will come to regular use in certain fields of social research. During the last twenty years or so, sociologists have been heavily engaged in studying the relation of social structure (family, occupation, age, and so on) to social life feelings and the like (estrangement, morale, alienation, and so on). In this work, they have tended to neglect—although there are conspicuous exceptions—the possibility that differences between social categories in reported social life feelings are mainly an effect of differences in responding desirably. As a minimum, RD16 directs attention to this possibility. It also directs attention to the possibility that response style is a form of social adaptation.

7

Evaluating
the Reliability
and Validity
of Social Life
Feeling Scales

This chapter is a critical evaluation of the twelve SLFSs plus a general comment on the prospects of social life feeling scales ever becoming standard in the field. We first review our efforts to interpret the SLFSs; second, we consider some conventional standards for judging scales and differences among the twelve SLFSs in meeting them; third, we give each scale a composite rating, taking into account both qualitative and quantitative characteristics. Lastly, we discuss factors working against movement toward standard social life feeling scales in sociology and thereby against strict comparisons between different populations in time and space.

Table 18. Twelve SLFSs: Best Item-Total Correlations; Statistically Closest Scales; Interpretations.

SLFS No.	Tape No.	Item	Item-Total r	Statistically Closest Scale	Correlation	Interpretation	Rating[a]
1	133	The future is too uncertain for a person to plan ahead	.49	Srole Anomia (9 items)	.78		
	62	What happens in life is largely a matter of chance	.47	Topic 4(N), Self-Determination	.83	Doubt that individual controls his destiny; skeptical about doctrine of individualism	C
	67	Nowadays a person has to live pretty much for today and let tomorrow take care of itself	.46	Subject class 3(N), Philosophy of Life	.75		
2	3	There are few people in this world you can trust, when you get right down to it	.57	Rosenberg Faith in People	.77		
	159	Too many people in our society are just out for themselves and don't really care for anyone else	.56	Topic 1(N), Trust	.75	Doubt that people are trustworthy; distrust of people	S
	13	Most people can be trusted	.56	Subject class 4(N), People	.86		
3	217	Very lonely or remote from other people	.53	Bradburn-Caplovitz Negative Self-Feeling	.84		
	221	Depressed or very unhappy	.53	Topic 13(N), Élan	.87	Feel down; negative affect; feel isolated	S

	Item	Text	Loading	Subscale	Rel.	Description	
	149	I feel that I'm not a part of things	.50	Subject class 1(N), Self	.90		
4	22	There is too little variety in my job	.50	Walker Worker-Morale	.67		
	34	I am satisfied with the work I do	.49	Topic 2(N), Work Morale	.85	Satisfied with job	C
	35	My job gives me a chance to do what I do best	.47	Subject class 2(N), Self-in-Situation	.79		
5	57	The average person has a great deal of influence on government decisions	.50	Smith Efficacy in Public Affairs	.78		
	53	The average citizen has considerable influence on politics	.48	Topic 3(P), Civic Morale	.85	Faith in role and importance of individual in government	C
	55	The average person has much to say about running local government	.41	Subject class 5(N), Institutions	.72		
6	88	I get a lot of fun out of life	.51	Rosenberg Depressive Affect	.72		

Table 18 (Cont.)

SLFS No.	Tape No.	Item	Item-Total r	Statistically Closest Scale	Correlation	Interpretation	Rating[a]
	144	Things get better for me as I get older	.49	Topic 5(P), Dejection	.73	Feel up; positive affect	S
	119	I am satisfied with the way things are working out for me	.47	Subject class 1(P), Self	.51		
7	159	Too many people in our society are just out for themselves and don't really care for anyone else	.44	Struening-Richardson Perceived Purposelessness	.80		S
	189	Many people don't know what to do with their lives	.39	Topic 10(N), Expediency	.55	Cynical about motives of others	
	175	Many people are friendly only because they want something from you	.37	Subject class 4(N), People	.66		
8	42	Most politicians are more interested in themselves than in the public	.48	Srole Anomia (5 items)	.61		
	43	I have little confidence in the government today	.42	Topic 3(N), Civic Morale	.81	Cynical about government and politicians; disenchanted with democracy	C
	208	In my opinion, this country is sick	.42	Subject class 5(N), Institutions	.90		
9	128	The future looks very bleak	.55	Rundquist-Sletto Morale	.75		

Factor	Item #	Item	Loading	Source	Loading	Description	Type[a]
	134	The future of this country is very uncertain	.51	Topic 8(N), Social Optimism	.80	Outlook on future, pessimistic to optimistic	C
	125	The lot of the average man is getting worse, not better	.47	Subject class 4(N), People	.69		
10	78	Poor people could improve their lot if they tried	.40	Struening-Richardson Alienation	.28		
	73	Individuals are poor because of the lack of effort on their part	.33	Topic 4(P), Self-Determination	.74	Feel that people have themselves to blame for their poor economic showing	S
	75	Anyone can raise his standard of living if he is willing to work at it	.32	Subject class 3(P), Philosophy of Life	.33		
11	194	I can't do much for other people	.39	Gurin Personal Control	.62		
	65	I have little influence over the things that happen to me	.38	Topic 4(N), Self-Determination	.63	Feel demoralized; matters seem hopeless; giving up	C
	191	I seem to be marking time these days	.37	Subject class 1(N), Self	.60		
12	E5	Worry about getting ahead	.48	Bradburn-Caplovitz Worries	.83		
	E3	Worry about work	.43	Topic 14 (N), Fears and Worries	.82	Concerned about making it	S
	E10	Worry about future	.42	(See page 68)			

[a]C = complex; S = simple.

The Question of Validity

In evaluating a scale, consideration must be given not only to reliability coefficients and the like but also to what is being measured by that scale. In the absence of an at least plausible answer to that question, a scale would seem to be practically useless. Why would one obtain and analyze scores corresponding to no well-defined variable? It is a fair question.

By way of answering this question, we here review and evaluate our efforts to interpret what it is the twelve SLFSs are measuring. After restating interpretations, we comment briefly on how they stand in respect to face validity and criterion validity.

Details pertinent to this discussion are given in Table 18. For each scale, we first give its three best items; next its closest author scale, closest topic scale, and closest subject-class scale; then what we take it to be measuring in a word or two, and a rating of that interpretation as simple or complex. A simple rating is a fairly obvious, not-too-debatable, easily reached interpretation; a complex rating is a not-too-obvious, probably debatable, and reached-with-some-difficulty interpretation.

Review of Interpretations. SLFS1 was taken initially to be a measure of social despair, or the tendency to see social circumstances as fairly hopeless—no cause for optimism, no understanding this world, tomorrow no better than today, future uncertain. Later, after reviewing its correlations with differently constructed tests—author, topic, subject class—and reexamining its contents in this new light, we dropped *social despair* in favor of *doubt about self-determination*. While the items do reflect despair in a general way, they seem to reflect more particularly a doubt about the doctrine that anyone can make it if he tries, or skepticism about the American creed of individualism. We did consider that SLFS1 might be a measure of anomie, since its correlation with Srole's Anomia Scale was the highest in that category. However, we rejected anomie as an interpretation because the items seemed to refer more directly to a feeling of little or no self-determination than to a feeling of self-to-other alienation.

SLFS2 was taken in the first place to be a measure of the feeling that people are generally untrustworthy; at that stage we called it *social distrust*. Its correlations with differently constructed tests suggested no change in interpretation—doubt that people can be trusted—but they did cause us to question our choice of title. After reexamining contents, we dropped *social distrust* for *doubt about trustworthiness of people*, this latter being a more precise description of what we had in mind.

SLFS3 was taken from the start as a measure of feeling down. We chose that term because it is relatively free of clinical connotations; it connotes a feeling that everyone in the population has to a greater or lesser degree. In this case, our reexamination of content and analysis of correlations suggested no change either in interpretation or in label.

SLFS4 was first interpreted as a measure of worker morale, mainly because it represented a subset of items on that topic. Later, on reexamining its contents, we took it to be a measure of job satisfaction—most of its items have the term *job* either as subject or in the predicate.

Perhaps a more refined interpretation is called for. Specialists on worker morale point out that a worker may be satisfied with some aspects of his job, dissatisfied with others. He may be satisfied with his responsibilities but not with his wages; he may be satisfied with what he is doing but not where he is doing it; and so on. From this viewpoint, there is not one job satisfaction but many.

But whatever the validity of such distinctions, the appearance of another scale on job satisfaction would seem to exemplify what has been deplored as bad practice—namely, constructing a new scale when good ones are already available. We certainly did not have a job satisfaction scale in mind when we planned this research. One appeared simply because many items on work satisfaction appeared willy-nilly in the content domain, and these items formed a statistical cluster, or scale.

SLFS5 was first interpreted as a measure of civic morale, chiefly because it consisted of items on that topic. By *civic morale* we meant a more or less positive (negative) feeling about government and politics. Later analysis suggested that *civic morale* was too broad and that *faith in citizen participation in American government* was closer to the feeling being measured by this scale. As in the case of job satisfaction, we did not set out to construct a scale on faith in political institutions; rather, that scale appeared because many items on this topic appeared willy-nilly in the domain, and some of these items met scale criteria.

SLFS6 presented relatively few problems in interpretation and labeling. At the start we took it to be measuring an aspect of psychological well-being—we called it *feeling up*. It might have been given a more technical title (say, *positive affect*); but here as elsewhere we decided in favor of the everyday term in order to focus on what we assume is the universality of feeling up. Everyone feels up now and then, although some persons to a greater degree than others.

We interpreted SLFS7 as a measure of the feeling that in their daily life people act not on the basis of what is fair and just but rather opportunistically on the basis of personal advantage. In the course of interpreting SLFS7 we left that interpretation unchanged but dropped the term *expediency*, which refers more to action than feeling, for *cynicism*, which refers more to feeling than action.

The interpretation of SLFS8 was narrowed in the course of analyzing its makeup. We first took it to be a measure of enthusiasm and support for government in general. SLFS8 probably reflects that enthusiasm and support, but it seems to reflect more precisely the feeling that few people manage to live up to the ideals of political democracy. We refer to this perceived gap between what people espouse and what they practice as *disillusionment with government*.

We initially took SLFS9 as a measure of pessimism, or the tendency to look on the dark side of things. However, a reexamination of its contents, coming after a review of its correlations with alternative scales, suggested that it was more a measure of feeling about the future than of pessimism about things generally—past, present, future. At one point we did consider renaming it *morale*, since its highest correlation was with the Rundquist-Sletto Morale Scale. However, we decided against that because the items suggested not a determination to persevere in the face of difficulty, as implied by *morale*, but simply a view of the future as dark or bright.

SLFS10's correlations with differently constructed scales were negligible and threw little or no light on what it was measuring. At the start we took it to be a measure of the feeling that level of economic attainment is a matter of individual effort and initiative, or the reverse, that individual effort makes very little difference in economic success. There was nothing in our review(s) of SLFS10 to suggest a different interpretation.

We initially took *SLFS11* as a measure of self-determination—the feeling that one determines what one is and does. Its relatively high correlation with scores based on items from Gurin's Personal Control Scale was in line with this interpretation. Later, after reviewing relevant findings, we concluded that SLFS11 was measuring not so much the feeling that one controls what happens (or the reverse) but rather the feeling that the situation is generally hopeless and one is helpless to do anything about it. We termed this feeling "demoralization."

At the start, we took *SLFS12* to be a measure of tendency to worry. In the course of analyzing it, we came to regard it as less a measure of that tendency and more a measure of concern about living up to one's social responsibilities—being a parent, being a spouse, earning a living, and so on. This revised interpretation was more in accord with the correlations between SLFS12 and such factors as age, marital status, and income. As one might expect on sociological grounds, persons of higher socioeconomic status show more concern with career problems than persons of lower status.

Validities. None of the twelve SLFSs had face validity in the strict sense that all its items referred directly to the concept it supposedly was measuring. However, some scales approximated this criterion more closely than others. Scales whose interpretations were rated simple generally had more face validity than scales whose interpretations were rated complex. SLFS1 is relatively weak in face validity, since few of its items refer directly to doubt about self-determination; in contrast, SLFS12 is relatively strong, since all its items (with one possible exception) express concern with career.

No SLFS had criterion validity in the strict sense of predicting an independent criterion of that feeling, since in no case was such a criterion available for comparison. The scales did discriminate between social categories (age, race, income, and so on), but those findings do not constitute criterion validity, since they assume what is in question—namely, that social categories differ in their social life feelings. It is sociologically reasonable that social categories would differ in their feelings, and our findings are in line with this expectation. Thus, the finding that SLFS1 discriminates among income groups is in line with expectation that economically successful persons will attach more importance to self-effort than the economically unsuccessful. But such differences are not a demonstration of criterion validity; they would be only if they had been previously established by other means.

Reliability and Dimensionality. Scale scores are usually judged by their reliability and dimensionality, as well as by their validity. Low reliability would seem to disqualify a scale from use in scientific work; scores based on items held together by one factor are simpler in their latent structure than scores based on items bound together by two or more factors and are correspondingly easier to interpret. Here we discuss these matters in a general way and how they may be taken into account in evaluating social life feeling scales. We also consider scales from the standpoint of their meaningfulness in the sampled population as indexed by the missing response rate.

Alpha reliability: It is possible to evaluate a scale's alpha reliability against 1.00—the theoretical upper limit—or against the range of alpha reliabilities for scales similar in content and form. Relative to 1.00, all twelve SLFSs are low; relative to the reliabilities of comparable scales, alpha reliabilities are at least average, taking the interval from 0.70 to 0.80 as average. There are exceptions: Nos. 7, 10, 11, and 12 all have reliabilities below 0.70, and any one of these might be rejected in a given problem for that reason. Of course all would be eliminated from use if the standard were set as high as, say, 0.85. With social life feeling scales and the like, one has to either make do with relatively low reliability or do without scales altogether. Since social life feelings, almost by definition, are less stable than intelligence and personality, it is not surprising that measures of those feelings are comparatively low in reliability.

Tucker-Lewis reliability coefficient: As with alpha reliability, the Tucker-Lewis reliability coefficient may be judged against its limiting value of 1.00 or against a norm that takes into account the nature of the data—in the present case, the element of chance in the responses to social life feeling items. The requirement that scale items have a Tucker-Lewis coefficient of 0.90 was based on the judgment that an appreciably higher figure was outside the realm of practical possibility. In that judgment we were apparently correct: only three of the scales in their present form would have survived a requirement that the Tucker-Lewis coefficient be, say, 0.95 or higher.

We might have ignored the Tucker-Lewis coefficient altogether and required instead that only one factor be statistically significant. But that criterion is as unrealistically high as a Tucker-Lewis coefficient of 0.95. Social life feeling items in groups of five or more usually show more than one statistically significant factor by LISREL methods (Jöreskog and Sörbom, 1978). One must either compromise on statistical significance or do without composite scales altogether. A Tucker-Lewis reliability coefficient of 0.90 is such a compromise: it assures a relatively strong first factor but does not guarantee that other factors are lacking in statistical significance. But even at this level of compromise, two scales (Nos. 2 and 7) were substandard.

Missing response rate: The late Margaret Mead once said that a polling of public opinion in a primitive society would be misguided because there is no public opinion in a truly primitive society. It would be possible to conduct a poll mechanically and tabulate the results—to ask questions and count answers. However, these frequencies would correspond to nothing but themselves.

Mead's caution against polling for opinions when none exist is a special case of the rule against asking meaningless questions in a survey. This rule has special relevance for social life feeling items, since such items may touch on matters about which most people have no feelings or only the vaguest ones. Statements such as "The world is too complicated for me to understand," "The future is too uncertain for a person to plan ahead," and "There are few people in this world you can trust, when you get right down to it"—all from SLFS1—may be meaningless in the sense that they pertain to matters about which people have practically no feelings (although they may give answers).

One indication of an item's meaningfulness in a sample of respondents is its missing response rate. An item's missing response rate is the number of responses per 100 for which a substantive response was missing, or the number of responses that could not be scored 0 or 1 before statistical estimation (see Appendix D). If seventy-six cases could not be scored on a given item, then that item's missing response rate was $76/1522 = 0.05 = 5.0$ percent. Other things being equal, a less meaningful item might be expected to have a higher missing response rate than a more meaningful one; and, by extension, a less meaningful SLFS might be expected to have a higher average (per item) missing response rate than a less meaningful one.

Missing response rates for scales are included in Table 19. They range from 1.2 to 6.8 around a mean (weighted) of 3.8 (percent). They provide an objective basis for rating scales by relevance to respondents. By this criterion SLFS3 is best and SLFS8 is worst. We note in passing that scales consisting of items about self drew fewer missing responses than scales consisting of items about society and by that criterion are better. A methodological implication is that the problem of correcting for missing data will be greater in studies based on items (or scales) about people in general than in studies based on items about self.

Summary Ratings. From the foregoing account, and details given elsewhere, it is clear that no scale was perfect in every respect or, for that matter, in any respect. Nor was any scale uniformly high or low in every detail. But some scales were higher than others on the average, suggesting that scales might be at least rated as superior, good, or fair, if not put in rank order, 1 through 12.

We undertook to do that, that is, to rate them as superior, good, or fair, but with misgivings—misgivings because scales differ in length and are therefore not strictly comparable and because it is impossible to average (in the ordinary sense) qualitative characteristics and quantitative coefficients. However, we felt it necessary to try, since the question whether one scale was better than another was bound to arise sooner or later.

General ratings were based on how well the scales performed in the following six categories: alpha reliability, Tucker-Lewis reliability, missing response rate, relation to social background, simplicity of meaning, and number of proxies (number of scales dropped in its favor). Table 19 gives both general ratings and the detail going into them. No scale was rated superior, simply because no scale seemed definitely superior to scales that rated no better than

Table 19. Twelve SLFSs, Evaluation Sheet.

SLFS	Number of Items	dα reliability	T-L reliability	MRR[a]	Largest PEV[b]	Interpretation[c]	Proxies[d]	Summary Evaluation
1	14	.80	.94	3.6	22.8	C	16	Good
2	8	.80	.86	3.3	7.3	S	14	Good
3	10	.80	.96	1.2	3.5	S	7	Good
4	9	.75	.92	2.9	7.8	C	5	Good
5	10	.71	.92	5.5	1.5	C	8	Fair
6	11	.75	.94	3.5	9.4	S	5	Good
7	6	.62	.87	3.2	1.9	S	—	Fair
8	9	.71	.96	6.8	6.6	C	—	Fair
9	12	.78	.96	4.8	10.0	C	11	Good
10	5	.53	.90	4.5	2.0	S	1	Fair
11	9	.66	.96	3.5	19.6	C	—	Good
12	6	.65	.91	1.4	22.7	S	2	Good

[a]Percent nonscorable responses on base of 1,522.
[b] One-factor percentage explained variance. See Chapter Five.
[c]C = complex, S = simple.
[d]As between two differently constructed scales with a correlation above 0.60, whichever has the higher reliability is proxy for the other. See Chapter Four for a full explanation.

good. In effect, we found it possible to classify scales only as more or less satisfactory, not to make finer distinctions within these two levels. Eight scales were rated good, and four were rated fair. It turned out, althought we did not plan it that way, that fair scales were below average in four or more categories, while good scales were above average in three or more. Fair scales were relatively low in reliability and weak in their relation to social background; they had relatively high missing response rates and relatively few proxies. By contrast, good scales were relatively high in reliability and strong in their relation to social background; they had relatively low missing response rates and had relatively many proxies (excepting SLFS11).

These general ratings—good or fair—must be taken with a certain reserve; they serve mainly to draw attention to scale limitations. They are arbitrary in the rating categories on which they rest and in the weights assigned to categories. They would change if evaluation categories were dropped and added—for example, if the statistical significance of the residual correlations were substituted for the Tucker-Lewis reliability coefficient. They would change if the weight of one category relative to another were changed—for example, if alpha reliability were given more weight and number of proxies less. By reason of this latter possibility, a different analyst reviewing the same evidence might come up with a different distribution of ratings, including the presence of superior one or more times.

Concluding Remarks. An implicit goal of this research was to develop scales that might become standard in the field. (By *standard scale* we mean a scale whose use is assumed in a given line of research unless there are special circumstances to the contrary.)

It is possible that one or more of the twelve SLFSs might become standard in the field. But whatever uses they may find, at the very least they bring out circumstances that have fostered ad hoc scales and worked against movement toward standard scales (in the field of sociology). The variety of scaling methods is one circumstance; uncertainty in the meaning of scale items is another—items may differ in meaning between populations and/or change in meaning within populations.

The variety of scaling methods has multiplied since Thurstone and Chave (1929) first proposed their equal-appearing interval scale in the late 1920s. In the early 1930s, Likert (1932) suggested a change in procedure that would make scaling less costly in time and energy. In the late 1930s, Guttman (1941) came up with a radically different model—the Guttman scale—and a method for fitting it. And in the middle 1940s Lazarsfeld (1950) formulated his latent-structure model with the Guttman scale as a special case. All of these added to the variety of scaling methods.

Just now structural equation models are in the spotlight. The method (LISREL) of Jöreskog and Sörbom (1978) is used in sociology today both to measure the relation of multiple indicators to the latent variable and the relation of the latent variable to its prior causes. A recent study by J. Miller and others (1979) supplies an example. Muthén (1979) has extended this method to the special case of dichotomous indicators, similar to those in our research. His broad strategy is to introduce the latent variable as an explicit term in the classical probit model (Finney, 1951), and then to incorporate that equation in a structural model. At present, several investigators (Duncan, in press; Reiser, 1981) are exploring the potentialities of the Rasch model (Lord and Novick, 1968, chap. 21) for measuring social attitudes and the like. But Muthén is the only researcher who has treated the latent variable as both the cause of its dichotomous indicators and the effect of its antecedent causes.

The structural equation approach has significantly changed the form of contemporary sociology; however, its promise for social measurement has yet to be demonstrated. If history repeats itself, it will be in demand for a time, only to be superseded by still later developments. To date the theory and method of scaling (Torgerson, 1967) has been in a state of flux. Although most observers would regard this flux as healthy, they would probably also concede that it has been a factor working against the emergence, possibly premature, of a few standard scales.

But probably a more basic factor working against standard social life feeling scales is the uncertain meaning of scale items, particularly their tendency to change in meaning from time to time and, in consequence, to change in the pattern of their interrelations. An item may lose all meaning in time; or it may reflect two feelings where before and when analyzed for the first time it reflected only one. As a result of such shifts, a scale by definition at the time of construction may be that in name only after a longer or shorter period. Items that scaled soldiers in World War II may not work on the soldiers in the next war.

The prospect of such breakdowns in scale patterns, attributable to the instability of items, has doubtless contributed to the tendency of sociologists to modify existing scales so as to better suit their purposes. That modification may consist in adding items or dropping items or both; and when items are both added and dropped, the modified scale may bear practically no resemblance to the original. This tendency, documented first for the period 1930–1970 (Appendix A), is present to a degree in the most recent work of sociologists. In a survey of the *American Sociological Review*, the *American Journal of Sociology*, the *Social Psychology Quarterly*, and *Social Forces* for the period 1976–1980, I counted thirty-two articles or research notes (comments were excluded) making use of items closely similar to those appearing in the twelve SLFSs. The sociological concern of these articles was generally the relation of social circumstance and mental attitude, as indicated by the following titles: "Life Satisfaction and Religion: A Reanalysis" (Hadaway, 1978); "Work Values and Job Rewards: A Theory of Job Satisfaction" (Kalleberg, 1977); "Black Ghetto Diversity and Anomie: A Sociopolitical View" (Kapsis, 1978); "Social Class and Psychological Distress" (Kessler and Cleary, 1980); "Occupational Structure and Alienation" (Kohn, 1976). A few articles were mainly methodological (for example, Zeller, Neal, and Groat, 1980; Gurin, Gurin, and Morrison, 1978).

Although in this sample of thirty-two studies, previously constructed scales were used intact with some regularity—particularly mental health indexes—the more common pattern was to modify a previously constructed scale in one or more ways: by dropping items, by adding items, by paraphrasing items, or by all three. Scales were constructed from scratch in at least six studies.

There was some work, not all appearing in the above-mentioned thirty-two articles, on trends in responding to exactly the same item from time to time. This work, at least some of it, may reflect the judgment that until SLF scales and the like are improved, it is better not to use them at all and instead to limit the analysis to items one at a time. While scales have their weaknesses, so do individual items. Problems of reliability and validity are not solved by analyzing items one at a time. Moreover, it is only by applying scaling methods to a large number of items all at a time that the utility of any one item either alone or in combination with others can be judged, whether by multiple scalogram analysis (Lingoes, 1963) or multiple factor analysis (Harman, 1967). Our research bears out this point.

Our research took as its point of departure the miscellany of social life feeling scales in American sociology. In the midst of this diversity we found considerable unity (by analyzing the relation of each item to every other). We found a close correspondence between our twelve empirical scales and the more numerous author scales. We took this to mean that sociologists have operationally distinguished no more than twelve social life feelings, however many nominal distinctions they have drawn, and that twelve scales would suffice for maintaining those operational distinctions.

We found that the twelve scales, but not equally so, tended to arrange themselves in clusters (Chapter Three), as if at another level of generality there are fewer than twelve distinctions. We interpreted this finding to mean that there are feelings more general than those corresponding to the twelve scales. In this speculative view, individual scales within clusters reflect both a general feeling and a specific feeling. Cynicism appears to be present in distrust of people (No. 2), faith in citizen participation (No. 5), motives of others (No. 7), and doubts about democracy (No. 8); fatalism seems to be present in doubts about self-determination (No. 1), economic attainment (No. 10), and feeling demoralized (No. 11); feeling estranged generally appears to be present in feeling down (No. 3), feeling upbeat (No. 6), and possibly job satisfaction (No. 4). These findings suggest that items within clusters might be regrouped and reweighted for possible measures of these conceptually more general feelings. In the meantime, the best scales within clusters might be used to represent these more general feelings.

Appendix A

Constructing
the Content Domain

The content domain in its final form consisted of 545 items appearing in a wide variety of scales for measuring social life feelings. Our first step in constructing it was to list terms denoting a social life feeling (for example, *optimistic, trustful, hopeful, demoralized, dispirited, disenchanted, helpful, powerless, useful, forgotten, isolated, lonely*). Second, we listed scales used in one way or another in sociology in measuring those concepts (for example, Rundquist-Sletto Morale Scale, Cumming's Morale Scale, Bradburn-Caplovitz Psychological Well-Being Questionnaire). Next, we listed all items appearing in those scales and questionnaires, and finally, we eliminated duplicate and extraneous items from that list.

Every scale on the list had a traceable link to an article appearing in the *American Sociological Review*, the *American Journal of Sociology, Social Forces,* or *Sociometry* (now the *Social Psychology Quarterly*) for the period 1930–1970. In thus limiting the pool, we risked missing eligible scales and/or items whose inclusion might have altered the pattern of our findings. We would probably have got a different collection of items if we had started with a different set of journals. Starting with the major sociological journals assured the inclusion of most scales in recent or current use in American sociology.

Searching for Scales

The search for scales took us to diverse specialties appearing in a wide variety of journals, monographs, reports, and reference books. Once begun, it followed no strict chronological sequence, and we generally found ourselves moving back and forth across periods of time within the same journal and also across different journals within the same period. In the course of collecting items, we examined over 407 references—and made contact with many more—located in over 100 journals and books. Of the 407 references, 308 appeared in social or behavioral science journals and the remaining 99 in books, monographs, abstracts, bulletins, catalogues, handbooks, and the like (for example, Miller, 1970).

Individual references did not, of course, contribute equally to our item pool. Some referred to scales but listed no items; some gave a few representative items from a given scale; some gave scales already on the list. Some references offered critical evaluations of existing scales, and these were carefully considered for their bearing on our own projected scales.

Screening Items

The bibliography of 407 entries encompassed over 140 distinct questionnaires, which together represented over 1,800 test items. This later total is greatly inflated by the presence of many items peripheral to our central concepts and many overlapping items between scales. Dropping both duplicate and extraneous items gave us a substantially smaller pool.

As a preliminary to screening individual items, we arbitrarily dropped all personality inventories and thereby reduced the total from 1,800 to 1,000 items approximately. In doing this, we did not automatically eliminate all items appearing in these inventories, since many of them also appeared in scales still on the list. By dropping personality tests, we in effect got rid of those items most distant from our central concern.

Next, also as a preliminary, we grouped the aforementioned 1,000 items by topical similarity. Our procedure was to determine the main topic of each item as best we could and assign items with equivalent topics to the same groupings. This operation produced sixteen groupings, covering many but not all of the items. Dropping the 171 unclassified items left us with a total of 823 items.

At this juncture, we wrote a number of "original" items, concentrating on the underrepresented topics, or topics with relatively few items. These new items were often no more than paraphrases of existing ones. Adding what appeared to be the best of these supplemental items raised the smaller frequencies somewhat but left the rank order of frequencies substantially unchanged; we had not succeeded in getting an even distribution of items across topics.

Also, at this stage, we dropped five topics from our classification and added three for a new total of fourteen categories. Topics were dropped either because they were peripheral to the core concepts or because they could plausibly be covered by some other category; categories were added to bring about a better alignment of items generally. The "final fourteen" are listed in Appendix B, together with the numerical representation of each in the national survey questionnaire.

Our next and last step in refining the item pool was to eliminate duplicates or near duplicates. Eliminating exact duplicates was a purely mechanical operation, but eliminating near duplicates was more complicated and involved considerable judgment. In handling near duplicates, our guiding principle was to represent no one theme by more than one item, regardless of syntactical differences among competing items. Eliminating duplicates and near duplicates reduced the total from 945 to 545. This pool of 545 was the source of items for both the pilot survey questionnaire and the national-sample survey questionnaire.

In the end, as stated before, the content domain gave the appearance of an orderly file of 545 relatively simple statements. But its orderliness at the end should not be permitted to obscure either its arbitrary makeup or its origin in practical social endeavor. Its makeup is arbitrary because it rests on somewhat arbitrary decisions about what to include; it is practical in origin because it grows out of broad social problems rather than theoretical issues.

Appendix B

Questionnaire Construction

In constructing the survey questionnaire, we had to decide which items to include from the longer list(s), since we could not include all; similarly, given the time available for the interview (approximately one hour), we had to decide which background items to include. We wanted to obtain as much background information as possible but not at the expense of a reliable representation of at least the list of 545 items if not the longer, unscreened list of around 1,000 (see Appendix A). This broad objective guided the design and construction of the national survey questionnaire.

Pilot Study

To help meet this criterion, we devised pilot questionnaires, A and B, and gave them to ninety-three and ninety-four randomly selected adults resident in Bloomington, Indiana. We had these specific questions in mind: (1) Do some items draw the same response from practically everyone and therefore have little or no value for discriminating between respondents? (2) Do some items, perhaps many, draw a substantial proportion of "don't knows" and by that criterion carry little meaning for the average respondent? (3) Do

144

respondents make frequent use of "strongly agree" and "strongly disagree" when presented along with "agree" and "disagree"? (4) How long does it take, on the average, for a respondent to answer a social life feeling item in a survey setting? The sense of these questions was to help fix the length of the questionnaire and to avert including practically useless questions and answers.

Each pilot form had 161 common items and 80 different items. Each respondent thus answered 241 items, not counting background questions. Together Forms A and B included 321 different items. Items were selected judgmentally in roughly proportional numbers from each of the fourteen topics into which items had been previously grouped and were split equally between keys within topics whenever possible. We deliberately chose items best meeting the criteria of simplicity, intelligibility, and brevity. For example, as between paired items with about the same meaning, we chose whichever was shorter and plainer. The distribution of all 321 scale items by topic is shown in Table 20, Column 1.

Table 20. 321 Pilot Survey Items by Topic;
237 National Survey Items by Topic and Key.

| | | | National Survey | |
Number	Topic	Pilot Survey	Agree	Disagree
1	Trust	26	11	9
2	Job morale	34	10	10
3	Civic morale	32	10	10
4	Self-determination	29	10	10
5	Dejection	16	4	6
6	Anomie	27	12	10
7	Social contentment	13	5	7
8	Social optimism	29	12	12
9	Social estrangement	29	12	12
10	Expediency	14	6	7
11	Despair	23	12	6
12	Social disenchantment	15	8	4
13	Élan	18	8	4
14	Worries	16	10	0
		321	130	107

Life feeling items were given in groupings of fifteen to twenty, with background items located between adjacent groups. Such a staggering of subject matter, it was thought, would break the monotony of the task and thereby help to hold respondent interest. To the degree possible, items were randomly assigned to groups and randomly arranged within groupings.

The sample plan called for one interview (adult) from each of 300 randomly selected households in the city of Bloomington, Indiana. We managed to get 187 cases. With more funds (person-hours) at our disposal, we might have brought this figure up to 250 households. We deliberately oversampled districts whose residents were below average in education on the supposition that relatively uneducated respondents would have more trouble with the questionnaire than educated respondents and that an analysis of these troubles would help us to improve the questionnaire. But in this endeavor we were not particularly successful: 80 percent of all respondents were high school graduates, and 39 percent were college graduates. This latter figure reflects the presence of university people everywhere in the municipal city and their generally greater willingness to participate in research projects.

In keeping with the purposes of the pilot study, we analyzed the respective distributions of "strongly agree" and "strongly disagree" proportions, the distribution of the modal proportions, and the distribution of the "don't know" proportions. We also calculated how long it took, on the average, to respond to a social life feeling item.

"Strongly agree" and "strongly disagree" were given as options on 48 of the 321 items (in addition to "agree" and "disagree"). The proportion choosing "strongly agree" ranged from 0.00 ("Friends are easy to find") to 0.21 ("Expect prices to keep going up"); the proportion choosing "strongly disagree" ranged from 0.00 ("Country is in for some hard times") to 0.25 ("Religion is more myth than truth"). The average proportion per item for "strongly agree" was .043; the average per item for "strongly disagree" was .076. Partly on the basis of these "use" statistics, but mainly for practical reasons (to save time, to simplify scoring, and so on), we decided against listing "strongly agree" and "strongly disagree" as options on the national survey questionnaire.

"Don't know" was given as an option on 256 of the 321 items, including the aforesaid 48 items with "strongly agree" and "strongly disagree." The proportion marking "don't know" ranged from 0.00 ("I have little in common with most people") to 0.33 ("Times are getting better"), around a mean value of 0.08. Approximately one third (84) of all 256 items had "don't know" proportions larger than 0.10. We made as little use of these 84 as possible, to avoid complications produced by "don't knows" (Schuman and Presser, 1978).

Modal frequencies (proportions) for the 208 agree/disagree items ranged from 0.48 ("Lot of average man does not change very much") to 0.98 ("Many things in life are worth while"); 41 items had a modal frequency larger than 0.80. To avert problems created by extreme marginals, we made as little use of these 41 as possible in our final questionnaire.

Scale items took around seven seconds (average) to answer, background items around twenty seconds. On the basis of these averages, we estimated that respondents could easily answer 250 social life feeling items in forty minutes or so and 50 background items in twenty minutes or so. But these time estimates turned out to be overly optimistic; in the national survey, respondents took more time per item.

National Survey Questionnaire

Our final questionnaire had 237 life feeling items, 30 items for measuring response sets, and 31 social background items. Social life feeling items were taken from the pilot questionnaire (rather than the longer list of 545) as a safeguard against including useless and ambiguous items.

The length of the questionnaire (number of questions) was fixed by the requirement that it take no more than one hour for a trained interviewer to give in the field. We arbitrarily decided to allot two thirds of the hour to scale items (including those for measuring response sets) and one third to the background items (sex, race, education).

We had initially planned to represent each topic by eighteen items, divided equally between keys. However, because of differences in the number and utility of items within topics, we were unable to adhere to this plan. Items were screened out if they got the same response from practically everyone and/or a high percentage of "don't knows," and these percentages were correlated to some degree with both topic and key. The unbalanced distribution of items by topic and key (Table 20, columns 2 and 3) is partly the result of these correlations.

Social background items were selected from those regarded by a panel of social scientists as most relevant for purposes of social and economic analysis (Van Dusen and Zill, 1975). Items for measuring response sets were taken from Jackson's Social Desirability Scale, Marlowe and Crowne's Social Desirability Scale, and Jackson and Messick's Acquiescing Scale (see Chapter Six).

In constructing the survey questionnaire, we worked closely throughout with the staff at Response Analysis, Inc., Princeton, New Jersey. They called our attention to defects in items; they advised substituting their wording on some background items for ours. They suggested that we separate items by general subject—noun or pronoun—and that we rotate the method of getting answers as a means of relieving the monotony of the interview.

In line with this last suggestion, we set up three ways of giving items (or getting answers):

Interview: "Now I am going to read you some statements that have been made about this country and its government. Please tell me whether you mostly agree or mostly disagree with each statement. Many of these issues are complicated, but we just want your first general impression on each statement."

Self: Interviewer hands respondent questionnaire and pen and then says: "Here are some statements that have been made about this country and its government. Please indicate whether you mostly agree or mostly disagree with each statement on the questionnaire by circling number '1' for 'agree' or number '2' for 'disagree.'" When respondent is finished, interviewer takes back questionnaire.

Card: Interviewer shuffles deck of cards and hands it to respondent along with sort board and then says: "The statements on these cards have been made about this country and its government. Please sort the cards on this board according to whether you mostly agree or mostly disagree with each statement." When respondent is finished, interviewer asks respondent to read the number of cards in each box. Unsorted cards are recorded "don't know."

Changing the order of methods across sections gave six different forms. These forms are listed in Table 21. Since forms were randomly assigned to respondents in equal numbers, each form was administered to approximately 250 respondents.

Table 21. Form of Administration by Section, Social Life Feeling Questionnaire.

		Form 1 White	Form 2 Blue	Form 3 Green	Form 4 Buff	Form 5 Yellow	Form 6 Pink
A	4	Interviewer-Administered Background Questions					
B	24	INT	CARD	SELF	INT	CARD	SELF
C	35	SELF	INT	CARD	SELF	INT	CARD
D	25	CARD	SELF	SELF	CARD	CARD	SELF
E	10	CARD	SELF	SELF	CARD	CARD	SELF
F	9	Interviewer-Administered Background Questions					
G	20	INT	CARD	INT	SELF	SELF	CARD
H	30	SELF	SELF	CARD	INT	CARD	INT
I	36	CARD	INT	SELF	CARD	INT	SELF
J	33	INT	CARD	INT	SELF	SELF	CARD
K	24	CARD	SELF	CARD	INT	INT	SELF
L	30	SELF	CARD	SELF	CARD	SELF	CARD
M	16	Interviewer-Administered Background Questions					
N	7	Postinterview Information					

Key: INT = Interviewer-administered.
CARD = Respondent card sort.
SELF = Self-administered.

Changing the method of giving items within the same questionnaire was done to break the monotony of the task (for interviewer as well as respondent); changing the sequence of methods across questionnaires enabled us to compare different methods—INT, CARD, SELF—on the same item. Our design thus answers to the question whether item marginals are significantly affected by form of administration. In a separate study, Newton, Prensky, and Schuessler (unpublished manuscript) concluded that "variations in form of administration may serve to reduce respondent (interviewer) fatigue and boredom, without significantly altering the results" (p. 16).

The questionnaire was put through three pretests by the staff at Response Analysis. The first edition, consisting of 269 scale items and 51 background items, was given to six adults resident in Princeton, New Jersey, in early May 1974. Scale items in random order were arranged in fifteen sections, with no two adjacent sections administered in the same way. The 51 background items were divided into three groups and placed at the beginning, in the middle, and at the end of the questionnaire. At issue were the length of the questionnaire and the feasibility of using different methods to get answers in the same interview. Getting answers by different methods from the same respondent seemed to pose no problems, but the questionnaire proved to be too long.

With the idea of cutting administration time, scale items were rearranged in seven groups of around 35 each, with background items interspersed as before. This second version was given to ten residents of Princeton, New Jersey, a week or so later. It was still too long, and at this juncture we decided to drop twenty of the background items; dropping background items seemed more consistent with our goals than giving up scale items.

The third version consisted of 268 scale items, divided into ten groups of 25 items per group, and 31 background items. This edition was given by members of RA's field staff to twenty-two residents in the Detroit metropolitan area in August 1974. Cases were chosen in accordance with Response Analysis's standard sampling plan, and respondents were approached and debriefed in the usual manner. Interviewers supplied evaluations on separate forms. On the basis of these evaluations, a small number of changes in wording were made, and one item was dropped because of its seeming ambiguity.

The questionnaire in its final form (available on request) called for 303 pieces of separate information. Herewith is a summary of its contents: Section A has four background items—household size, newspaper reading, political party, and political leaning. Sections B and C consist of twenty-four and thirty-five agree/disagree scale items, respectively, with the method of answering questions in C differing from the method for B.

Section D has twenty-five multiple-choice scale items: often, sometimes, seldom, and never. These items are answered by either SELF or CARD but not both, and in no case by INT. Section E also consists of multiple-choice scale items (ten), and, like D, it makes no use of INT; however, as with D, there is a change in form of administration between D and E. All ten items in E are on everyday worries.

Section F, coming after ninety-four scale items, has nine background items, mainly on respondent's employment. These background items are not self-administered.

Sections G, H, I, J, and K have twenty, thirty, thirty-six, thirty-three, and twenty-four agree/disagree scale items, respectively, with no two adjacent sections having the same form of administration. Section L consists of thirty items taken from three scales for measuring response sets: Jackson's SD scale; Jackson and Messick's Acquiescing Scale; Marlowe-Crowne Social Approval Scale. All thirty are answered true or false, as in the scales from which they are taken.

Section M consists of sixteen background items on education, marital status, and religion. As with A and F, none of these sixteen is self-administered. Section N consists of seven postinterview items: sex and race of respondent; day, hour, and length of interview; and two items on respondent's cooperation.

From the face sheet, which was a log of the interview, it was possible to establish the sex, race, education, and age of the interviewer, and with this information it was possible to investigate the correlation between interviewer characteristics and response patterns.

Appendix C

Sampling
and Interviewing

The survey population was defined as all persons eighteen years of age or older resident in households in the continental United States at the time of the survey (September 1974). The sample was defined as a random sample of 1,500 persons from that population. The sampling plan called for one randomly chosen adult from each of 1,500 randomly drawn households. Both sampling and interviewing were done by Response Analysis, Inc., Princeton, New Jersey.

In the first phase of sampling, households were selected with equal probabilities; in the second, respondents were randomly selected within households with probabilities inversely proportional to household size.

Households were drawn at each of 200 sample points (locations) in such numbers as to yield the sample quota of 1,500. It was supposed at the start that 10 assignments (drawings) would yield 7 completed cases and that 2,150 assignments would yield slightly more than 1,500 cases. But owing to a lower-than-expected completion rate, it became necessary to enlarge the number of assignments from 2,150 to 2,657. For all 2,657 drawings, no household was present in 152 cases. Of the 2,505 cases with household present, 1,522 yielded an interview, while 983 did not yield an interview. We sometimes refer to these 983 as the missing cases. (Breakdown of missing cases by cause available on request.)

The relatively low completion rate (1522/2505 = 0.608) was ascribed by Response Analysis to both the length of the questionnaire and its content, which was apparently uninteresting to many potential respondents. They stated: "Every reasonable effort was made to achieve as high a completion rate as possible. People cannot be forced to respond to survey interviews; they must be persuaded. We have found that, for general public studies, the most important factors affecting completion rates are interview length, subject matter, and perceived importance of the research. In all of these respects, your interview was more difficult than most. The interview length averaged 68 minutes, and the subject matter was not at all compelling from the respondent's point of view."

There were 187 interviewers on the national survey. They received no special training for this project, but almost all had attended at least one of the classes held periodically by Response Analysis for their interviewers. Some had attended as many as four classes.

Each interviewer had to complete satisfactorily at least one practice interview before being cleared to start work in the field. Practice interviews were sent to the home office (Princeton, N.J.) for critical review by staff; afterward, they were returned with comment to interviewers along with their survey assignments. Some interviewers were contacted by telephone to make sure they fully understood what they were doing. Interviewers not satisfactorily completing the practice assignment were dropped from the project.

Most interviewers were women (180 of 187), and most were white (173 of 187). All 7 men were white, and they accounted for 43 of all 1,522 cases (2.8 percent); all 14 blacks were women, and they accounted for 94 cases, or 6.2 percent. All interviewers were at least high school graduates, and 102 (55 percent) had had at least some college. They ranged in age from eighteen to sixty-seven around a median of forty-five years. Since the vast majority of interviewers were white women, it was virtually impossible to test for the effect of sex and race on pattern of response. However, differences in age and education made it possible to study the possible dependence of response patterns on these factors. (We found practically no such dependency.)

Interviewers differed in their work load; for some it was heavy, for others it was light. At the light end, 56 of the 187 interviewers did five interviews or fewer for a total of 202 cases (13.5 percent); at the heavy end, 7 interviewers did 20 or more for a total of 484 cases (31.8 percent). Such extreme groups may be compared on the pattern of responses they elicited, but we did not pursue this lead.

Interviewer experience was broken down by census region and community size (detail available on request). There was some variation across both classifications. Completion rates by region ranged from a high of 74.7 percent in East South Central to a low of 52.8 percent in Pacific. Smaller metropolitan areas (in population) had higher completion rates than larger, and nonmetropolitan areas had higher completion rates than metropolitan. While refusals were first in importance as a cause of no interview generally, they were second in importance to no one at home in South Atlantic. Similarly, refusals were proportionately less frequent in smaller metropolitan areas than in larger.

We note in passing that while sample distributions for classifications such as age and race were altered after adjusting for regional differences in the completion rate, marginal distributions for scale items one at a time and correlations between items two at a time were generally unaffected by that adjustment. Consequently, scales based on unweighted and weighted marginals differed very little in their means, standard deviations, and interitem correlations.

Appendix D

Adjusting the Data

The sample of 1,522 cases as just described presented two procedural questions: (1) whether cases should be differentially weighted so as to approximate their distribution(s) under sampling more nearly random and (2) whether cases with "missing values" (on a given variable) should be dropped or kept with an estimated value. In the end, we decided in favor of an analysis of an unweighted sample with estimated missing values. This decision, which has its pros and cons, was based on a finding of little or no difference between unweighted and weighted cases on either scale item means or interitem correlations and, similarly, a finding of little or no difference between missing values deleted and missing values estimated. Since the scheme of unweighted cases with estimated missing values presented fewer computing problems, we adopted that more convenient and economical procedure.

Weighted and Unweighted Cases

The sample had been weighted by Response Analysis, Inc., to compensate for inequalities in regional and household selection. We investigated the effect of that weighting relative to no weighting (or

155

the other way around) on both background variables and social life feeling items.

We compared distributions for weighted and unweighted samples on household size, age, marital status, race, sex, education, political party preference, and attitude of interviewee toward interview. Generally speaking, matched distributions were quite similar, with one predictable exception: the weighted sample necessarily had more large households than the unweighted and had correspondingly fewer small households. However, this difference was merely a consequence of weighting by size of household.

Otherwise, differences between distributions were slight, although not equally so, as indicated by the following detail: weighting gave more representation to persons under thirty years of age and to persons over sixty, and necessarily less to persons between those ages; it gave more representation to the currently married and less to the widowed; more to persons going further than high school, less to persons not completing high school; more to Republicans and Democrats, less to Independents. All in all, weighting (relative to no weighting) appeared to make some difference on background variables but not very much. The young and the old in large households gained at the expense of persons in their middle years in small households.

Scale Items

From the differences between weighted and unweighted cases on age, sex, education, and the like, it was not possible to predict the magnitude of their differences on scale item marginals. In such differences, the greater weight accorded one category may be nullified by the greater weight accorded another. The percentage of keyed responses on a given item ("The future looks bleak") might be raised by more weight to men but lowered by more weight to persons with college background, for example. On analyzing the difference distribution for 232 dichotomized items, we found only negligible differences. Approximately 75 percent of the differences between unweighted and weighted percent "agree" were smaller than 1 percentage point, and practically all were smaller than 2 percentage points. Similarly, 80 percent of the differences between unweighted and weighted percent "disagree" were smaller than 1 percentage point, and practically none was larger than 2 percentage points. Almost all (99 in 100) of the differences between unweighted and weighted percent "don't know" were smaller than 1 percentage point; none of the differences between unweighted and weighted percent "other" was larger than 1 percentage point.

For all differences combined, 85 out of 100 were smaller than 1 percentage point, and none was larger than 2.5. Although differences within response categories (agree, disagree, don't know, other) were not centered exactly on zero, the tendency away from zero was relatively weak. These results imply that composite scores, or summary measures, for unweighted and weighted cases will be closely similar in their distributions.

Scale Averages and Correlations

This prediction was generally borne out by an analysis of eighty-one different scales, or composites. Here, because they are typical, we report findings on ten so-called author scales (see Chapter Four). Table 22 gives the mean score for each of these ten scales for both weighted and unweighted cases, as well as the standard deviation. The numerical similarity between means and standard deviations in these comparisions is not so remarkable when one considers the tendency of differences on items individually to center on zero. The net difference between weighted and unweighted cases on composites of such items will necessarily be smaller than the difference between weighted and unweighted cases for any single item. Our findings are in line with this statistical requirement.

To extend the analysis, we obtained the differences between weighted and unweighted cases on all forty-five interscale correlations. In this comparison, we found that correlations were slightly larger in the weighted sample, that approximately 85 percent of all differences were smaller than 0.02, and that none was larger than 0.04. From this comparison, as well as similar ones, we concluded that composite scores (scores based on two or more items) for weighted and unweighted samples were practically identical.

It should be borne in mind that our finding of no difference between weighted and unweighted samples holds for one particular

**Table 22. Means and Standard Deviations for Ten Author Scales,
Weighted and Unweighted Cases.**

Author	Title	Mean		Standard Deviation	
		U	W	U	W
Sletto	Morale	5.13	5.06	2.16	2.16
Srole	Anomia	5.23	5.06	2.49	2.47
Cumming	Morale	2.14	2.09	1.49	1.48
Dean	Isolation	2.59	2.60	1.57	1.56
Langner	Mental Health	1.99	1.99	1.60	1.59
Bradburn	Well-Being	3.56	3.56	2.14	2.13
Struening	Purposelessness	3.51	3.51	1.31	1.31
Struening	Alienation	6.00	5.95	2.60	2.60
Neal	Isolation	2.51	2.50	1.44	1.45
Aiken	Alienation	2.54	2.51	1.80	1.78

Note: See Chapter Four for bibliographic detail.

weighting scheme. With a different weighting scheme, we might have got quite different results. Although a standard weight scheme would have many advantages, especially in comparative sociological work, at present no such scheme is in use, and to the best of my knowledge none has been proposed.

Estimating Missing Values

In "taking the test," respondents were forced to choose between "agree" and "disagree" on 202 items; between "true" and "false" on 30 items; and among "often," "sometimes," "seldom," and "never" on 35 items. But respondents, as one would expect, did not always choose one of the prescribed answers. In some instances, they gave no answer; in some, they said they did not know; in other instances, they said they were uncertain or undecided; and occasionally they said the question was unclear or meaningless.

The frequency of these deficient responses (deficient in the sense that they could not be scored) is brought out by Table 23, which gives the distribution of the missing (deficient) response rate for 237 items by questionnaire section. The mean rate for all items was 3.35, with considerable variation in means between sections. For

Table 23. Missing Response Rates by Questionnaire Section

Class Interval	Total	B	C	D-E	G	H	I	J	K
0.0-0.9	29	0	0	15	12	0	1	0	1
1.0-1.9	44	0	1	20	3	9	6	0	5
2.0-2.9	45	0	9	0	2	7	8	10	9
3.0-3.9	40	1	13	0	1	7	7	4	7
4.0-4.9	28	3	6	0	1	4	7	7	0
5.0-5.9	23	5	3	0	0	1	5	8	1
6.0-6.9	13	5	0	0	1	2	2	3	0
7.0-7.9	8	4	3	0	0	0	0	1	0
8.0-8.9	4	3	0	0	0	0	0	0	1
9.0-9.9	3	3	0	0	0	0	0	0	0
Total	237	24	35	35	20	30	36	33	24
Mean	3.35	6.71	3.87	1.07	1.50	3.01	3.48	4.27	2.85

example, the mean rate for the 24 items of Section B was 6.71, compared with a mean rate of 1.07 for the 35 items of Sections D and E. Such differences are probably due not to differences in position in the questionnaire but rather to differences in the subject class of items between sections. Section B consists mainly of assertions about society, and such statements generally drew more deficient responses than assertions about self; sections D and E consist almost entirely of assertions about self.

In a different view, Table 23 gives the number of deficient responses that would have to be made up (estimated) in order that no case have a missing item (or no item a missing case). This number is approximately 10 responses in every 300. Since this number is relatively small, and since deleting cases is practically inconvenient, we elected to estimate missing values in some systematic fashion.

We considered two possibilities: (1) assigning item means means = proportion of keyed responses) to deficient replies or (2) replacing deficient responses by responses chosen with probabilities proportional to item means (for example, making the probability of choosing the keyed response equal to 0.60 if the item mean was 0.60). We more or less rejected the first scheme out of hand for the reason that it is at odds with the principle that all responses be scored in the same way. When the item mean is used to replace a deficient response, some responses are scored 0 or 1, while others get a value somewhere in between 0 and 1. Under this scheme, strict binary scoring is dropped in favor of 0, X, 1 scoring, X being reserved for the missing or defective replies. In contrast, estimating responses with probabilities proportional to marginals maintains a single scoring system. It also tends to maintain the mean and the standard deviation. However, it tends to deflate the correlation coefficient, but not by much when the proportion of missing data is slight, since the absence of correlation (independence) between estimated responses will carry little weight when the number of such estimates is small.

To confirm this tendency toward smaller correlations (which is akin to attenuation by measurement error), we set up the distribution of product-moment correlation coefficients based on a pairwise deletion procedure, and the distribution of correlation coefficients based on observed and estimated responses combined; then we calculated the differences between corresponding coefficients and set up their distribution. Pairwise deletion correlations were slightly larger on the average than what we came to call the nomiss correlations (correlations based on no missing values), but the difference was negligible (mean difference = 0.005). It is this finding that supplies a justification for replacing deficient responses by responses drawn with probabilities proportional to observed marginals.

Concluding Remark

It is understood that our findings hold only for our methods and for our sample. The slight difference between the pairwise deletion and nomiss correlations is due to the relatively low missing response rate (3.35) and would necessarily increase with an increase in the missing response rate. Similarly, weighted and unweighted samples would differ in their item marginals if groups extreme in their social life feelings were screened out by assigning them zero weights. A standardization method akin to the standard million of demography would be useful in this line of work.

Appendix E

Statistical Formulas

Phi-coefficient

The product-moment correlation coefficient between two binary (0, 1) variables has come to be known as the phi-coefficient. It may be calculated from the cell frequencies of a fourfold table as follows:

$$r_\phi = \frac{ad - bc}{\sqrt{(a + b)(c + d)(a + c)(b + d)}} \qquad (1)$$

where a = number of cases with $X = 1$, $Y = 1$ as coordinates; b = number with $X = 0$, $Y = 1$; c = number with $X = 1$, $Y = 0$; d = number with $X = 0$, $Y = 0$.

Its maximum value may be calculated from marginal frequencies as follows:

$$\max r_\phi = \sqrt{\frac{L}{N - L} \times \frac{N - M}{M}} \qquad (2)$$

where L = the largest marginal frequency, M = the next-largest frequency, and N = the total number of cases. When marginals are identical, max r_ϕ = 1.00; otherwise it is less than 1.00. Replacing r_ϕ by $r_\phi/\text{max } r_\phi$ may be justified in some problems; for a discussion of the issues, see Carroll (1961); also Horst (1965).

Tetrachoric Correlation Coefficient

The tetrachoric correlation coefficient is an estimate of the product-moment correlation between two normally distributed variables. It is based on the cell frequencies of a fourfold table. With 50:50 marginals $(a + b = c + d = a + c = b + d)$, it is given by the formula

$$r_t = \sin\left\{90° \cdot \frac{(a + d - b - c)}{N}\right\} \tag{3}$$

otherwise it takes the form

$$r_t = \cos\left\{180° \cdot \frac{\sqrt{bc}}{\sqrt{ad} + \sqrt{bc}}\right\} \tag{4}$$

The validity of both (3) and (4) rests on the assumption that the fourfold table of cell frequencies corresponds to the division of a normal correlation table (surface) into four sectors. These formulas do not apply to variables that are skewed in their distributions.

Basing composite measures on tetrachoric coefficients may be justified in some cases. For a discussion of the issues, see Kim and Rabjohn (1979).

Point Biserial Coefficient

This coefficient is the product-moment correlation between a binary variable (X) and a continuous variable (Y). It is usually written as the regression coefficient of Y on X, weighted by the ratio of the standard deviation of X to the standard deviation of Y. In symbols:

$$r_b = (\bar{Y}_0 - \bar{Y}_1) \frac{\sigma_x}{\sigma_y} \qquad (5)$$

where $\bar{Y}_0$ and $\bar{Y}_1$ are group means, σ_x = standard deviation of X, σ_y = standard deviation of Y. Since r_b is a special case of the correlation ratio, it may be readily calculated from an analysis of variance of Y arranged by X. In this view, it is simply

$$r_b = \sqrt{\frac{\text{between-groups sum of squares}}{\text{total sum of squares}}} \qquad (6)$$

Coefficient Alpha

Coefficient alpha is a conservative measure of test reliability (Lord and Novick, 1968). It is usually written

$$\alpha = \frac{k}{k-1} \left(1 - \frac{\Sigma s_i^2}{s_x^2}\right) \qquad (7)$$

where k = number of test items; X = total score; X_i = score on ith item; s_x^2 = total score variance; s_i^2 = score variance of ith item.

A convenient approximation to (7) is given by

$$\alpha = \frac{k\bar{r}_{ij}}{1 + (k-1)\,\bar{r}_{ij}} \qquad (8)$$

where $\bar{r}$ = the mean interitem correlation coefficient. The relation of coefficient alpha to Armor's (1974) coefficient theta and to Heise and Bohrnstedt's (1970) coefficient omega is given in Greene and Carmines (1979). For the twelve social life feeling scales, alpha, theta, and omega are practically identical.

Coefficient of Concordance

This coefficient is a measure of agreement among a set of m rankings. Kendall and Buckland (1960) give this definition: If m rankings of n objects are arranged one under another and the rankings summed for each of the n objects, and if S is the sum of squares of deviations of these sums from their common mean $1/2\, m\, (n + 1)$, the coefficient of concordance W is

$$W = \frac{12S}{m^2\,(n^3 - n)} \tag{9}$$

The mean rank-order correlation between rankings two at a time $\bar{R}$ is connected to W by the following equation:

$$\bar{R} = \frac{mW - 1}{m - 1} \tag{10}$$

$\bar{R}$ may be larger or smaller than W.

Factor Analysis

The model of factor analysis is the weighted sum (Harman, 1967)

$$z_j = a_{j1}F_1 + a_{j2}F_2 + \ldots + a_{jm}F_m + d_jU_j \qquad (j = 1,2, \ldots ,n) \tag{11}$$

The problem of factor analysis is to solve for the a_{ij} on the right-hand side of (11) from the observed values on the left-hand side. One solution is given by the eigenvalues of the correlation matrix and their corresponding eigenvectors. A related solution is given by the likelihood function (Lawley and Maxwell, 1963). When principal-factor and ML loadings are calculated on the assumption that the number of common factors (m) is 1, the two solutions are identical. The practical significance of this result for present purposes is that principal-factor and ML loadings for items within scales (Chapter Two) are equal in their magnitudes.

Tucker-Lewis Reliability Coefficient

Tucker and Lewis (1973) show that the mean square for $n(n - 1)/2$ zero-order correlations squared has as its expected value

$$\xi(M_0) = \alpha_m + \delta_m + (1/n'_m) \tag{12}$$

where

$$n'_m = N - 1 - \frac{1}{6}(2n + 5) - \frac{2}{3}m$$

The mean square for the corresponding partial correlations on m common factors has as its expectation

$$\xi(M_m) = \delta_m + \frac{1}{n'_m} \tag{13}$$

Tucker and Lewis's reliability coefficient is by definition the percentage reduction in the total covariance attributable to m common factors,

$$\rho_m = \frac{\alpha_m}{\alpha_m + \delta_m} \tag{14}$$

An estimate is provided by

$$\rho_m \doteq \frac{M_0 - M_m}{M_0 - 1/n'_m} \tag{15}$$

About their coefficient they state (p. 5): "It may be interpreted as indicating how well a factor model with m common factors represents the covariances among the attributes of a population of objects. Lack of fit would indicate that the relations among the attributes are more complex than can be represented by m common factors." Their formulas rest on the assumption that the n variables follow a multivariate normal distribution.

References

Aiken, M., Ferman, L., and Sheppard, H. *Economic Failure, Aliena-tion, and Extremism.* Ann Arbor: University of Michigan Press, 1968.

American Journal of Sociology, 1941, *47.*

American Psychological Association. *Standards for Educational and Psychological Tests.* Washington, D.C.: American Psychological Association , 1974.

Andrews, F. M., and Withey, S. B. *Social Indicators of Well-Being.* New York: Plenum, 1976.

Annals of the American Academy of Political and Social Science, 1941, *216;* 1942, *220.*

Arminger, E. *Faktorenanalyse.* Stuttgart, Germany: Teubner, 1979.

Armor, D. J. "Theta Reliability and Factor Scaling." In H. Costner (Ed.), *Sociological Methodology 1973-1974.* San Francisco: Jossey-Bass, 1974.

Block, J. *The Challenge of Response Sets.* New York: Appleton-Century-Crofts, 1965.

Bradburn, N. *The Structure of Psychological Well-Being.* Chicago: Aldine, 1969.

167

Bradburn, N., and Caplovitz, D. *Reports on Happiness: A Pilot Study of Behavior Related to Mental Health.* Chicago: Aldine, 1965.

Bradburn, N., Sudman, S., and Associates. *Improving Interview Method and Questionnaire Design: Response Effects to Threatening Questions in Research.* San Francisco: Jossey-Bass, 1979.

Carr, L. E. "The Srole Items and Acquiescence." *American Sociological Review,* 1971, *36,* 287-293.

Carroll, J. B. "The Nature of the Data, or How to Choose a Correlation Coefficient." *Psychometrika,* 1961, *26,* 347-372.

Cartwright, D. S. "A Misapplication of Factor Analysis." *American Sociological Review,* 1965, *30,* 249-251.

Cavan, R., and others. *Personal Adjustment in Old Age.* Chicago: Science Research Associates, 1949.

Cherline, A., and Reeder, L. G. "The Dimensions of Psychological Well-Being." *Sociological Methods and Research,* 1975, *4,* 189-214.

Child, I. L. "Morale: A Bibliographical Review." *Psychological Bulletin,* 1941, *38,* 393-420.

Comrey, A. L., and Levonian, E. "A Comparison of Three Point Coefficients in Factor Analysis of MMPI Items." *Educational and Psychological Measurement,* 1958, *18,* 739-755.

Conklin, J. E. "Dimensions of Community Response to the Crime Problem." *Social Problems,* 1971, *18,* 373-385.

Converse, P. E. "The Nature of Belief Systems in Mass Publics." In D. E. Apter (Ed.), *Ideology and Discontent.* New York: Free Press, 1964.

Cumming, E., Dean, L. R., and Newell, D. S. "What is 'Morale'? A Case History of a Validity Problem." *Human Organization,* 1958, *17,* 3-8.

Dean, D. "Alienation: Its Meaning and Measurement." *American Sociological Review,* 1961, *26,* 753-758.

Dodder, R. A. "A Factor Analysis of Dean's Alienation Scale." *Social Forces,* 1969, *48,* 252-256.

Dohrenwend, B. P., and Crandall, D. L. "Some Relations Among Psychiatric Symptoms, Organic Illness, and Social Class." *American Journal of Psychiatry,* 1967, *3,* 1527-1538.

Dohrenwend, B. P., and Dohrenwend, B. S. *Social Status and Psychological Disorder: A Causal Inquiry.* New York: Wiley Interscience, 1969.

Duncan, O. D. "Rasch Measurement in Survey Research: Further Examples and Discussion." In C. F. Turner and E. Martin (Eds.), *Survey Measurement of Subjective Phenomena*. Washington, D.C.: National Research Council, in press.

Edwards, A. L. *The Social Desirability Variable in Personality Assessment and Research*. New York: Holt, Rinehart and Winston, 1957.

Finney, D. J. *Probit Analysis*. (2nd ed.) Cambridge: Cambridge University Press, 1951.

Gove, W. R., and Geerken, M. R. "Response Biases in Surveys of Mental Health: An Empirical Investigation." *American Journal of Sociology*, 1977, *82*, 1289–1317.

Greene, V. L., and Carmines, E. G. "Assessing the Reliability of Linear Composites." In K. F. Schuessler (Ed.), *Sociological Methodology 1980*. San Francisco: Jossey-Bass, 1979.

Groat, H. T., and Neal, A. G. "Social Psychological Correlates of Urban Fertility." *American Sociological Review*, 1967, *32*, 945–959.

Gurin, P., Gurin, E., and Morrison, B. M. "Personal and Ideological Aspects of Internal and External Control." *Social Psychology*, 1978, *41*, 275–296.

Gurin, P., and others. "Internal-External Control in the Motivational Dynamics of Negro Youths." *Journal of Social Issues*, 1969, *25*, 29–53.

Guttman, L. "The Quantification of a Class of Attributes." In P. Horst (Ed.), *The Prediction of Personal Adjustment*. New York: Social Science Research Council, 1941.

Hadaway, C. "Life Satisfaction and Religion: A Reanalysis." *Social Forces*, 1978, *57*, 636–643.

Harman, H. H. *Modern Factor Analysis*. Chicago: University of Chicago Press, 1967.

Heise, D. R., and Bohrnstedt, G. W. "Validity, Invalidity, and Reliability." In E. F. Borgatta and G. W. Bohrnstedt (Eds.), *Sociological Methodology 1970*. San Francisco: Jossey-Bass, 1970.

Horst, P. *Factor Analysis of Data Matrices*. New York: Holt, Rinehart and Winston, 1965.

Jackman, M. R. "Social Mobility and Attitude toward the Political System." *Social Forces*, 1972, *50*, 462–472.

Jackson, D. N. *Personality Research Form Manual*. Goshen, N.Y.: Research Psychologists Press, 1967.

Jackson, D. N., and Messick, S. "Acquiescence and Desirability as Response Determinants on the MMPI." *Educational and Psychological Measurement*, 1961, *21*, 771-790.

Jörsekog, K. G., and Sörbom, D. *Lisrel IV, a General Computer Program for Estimation of Linear Structural Equation Systems by Maximum Likelihood Methods*. Uppsala, Sweden: University of Uppsala, 1978.

Kalleberg, A. L. "Work Values and Job Rewards: A Theory of Job Satisfaction." *American Sociological Review*, 1977, *42*, 124-143.

Kapsis, R. E. "Black Ghetto Diversity and Anomie: A Sociopolitical View." *American Journal of Sociology*, 1978, *83*, 1132-1153.

Kendall, M. G., and Buckland, W. R. *A Dictionary of Statistical Terms*. Edinburgh, Scotland: Oliver and Boyd, 1960.

Kessler, R. C., and Cleary, P. D. "Social Class and Psychological Distress." *American Sociological Review*, 1980, *45*, 463-478.

Kim, J., and Rabjohn, J. "Binary Variables and Index Construction." In K. F. Schuessler (Ed.), *Sociological Methodology 1980*. San Francisco: Jossey-Bass, 1979.

Kohn, M. L. "Occupational Structure and Alienation." *American Journal of Sociology*, 1976, *82*, 111-130.

Kohn, M. L., and Schooler, C. "Class, Occupation, and Orientation." *American Sociological Review*, 1969, *34*, 659-678.

Langner, T. S. "A Twenty-Two Item Screening Score of Psychiatric Symptoms Indicating Impairment." *Journal of Health and Human Behavior*, 1962, *3*, 269-276.

Lawley, D. N., and Maxwell, E. A. *Factor Analysis as a Statistical Method*. London: Butterworths, 1963.

Lazarsfeld, P. F. "The Logical and Mathematical Foundation of Latent Structure Analysis." In S. A. Stouffer (Ed.), *Measurement and Prediction*. Princeton, N.J.: Princeton University Press, 1950.

Lenski, G. E., and Leggett, J. C. "Caste, Class and Deference in the Research Interview." *American Journal of Sociology*, 1960, *65*, 463-467.

Likert, R. "A Technique for the Measurement of Attitudes." *Archives of Psychology*, 1932, No. 140.

Lingoes, J. C. "Multiple Scalogram Analysis: A Set-Theoretical

Model for Analyzing Dichotomous Items." *Educational and Psychological Measurement*, 1963, *23*, 501–523.

Lord, F. M., and Novick, M. R. *Statistical Theories of Mental Test Scores.* Reading, Mass.: Addison-Wesley, 1968.

Lowenthal, M. F. "Social Isolation and Mental Illness in Old Age." *American Sociological Review*, 1964, *29*, 54–70.

Lystad, M. H. *Social Aspects of Alienation: An Annotated Bibliography.* Washington, D.C.: U.S. Government Printing Office, 1972.

McClosky, H., and Schaar, J. H. "Psychological Dimensions of Anomy." *American Sociological Review*, 1965, *30*, 14–40.

Marlowe, D., and Crowne, D. P. "A New Scale of Social Desirability Independent of Psychopathology." *Journal of Consulting Psychology*, 1960, *24*, 349–354.

Marx, G. *Protest and Prejudice: A Study of Belief in the Black Community.* New York: Harper & Row, 1967.

Messick, S. "Response Sets." In *International Encyclopedia of the Social Sciences* (Vol. 13). New York: Macmillan, 1968.

Messick, S. *Test Validity and the Ethics of Assessment.* Princeton, N.J.: Educational Testing Service, 1979.

Miller, D. C. *Handbook of Research Designs and Social Measurement.* (2nd ed.) New York: McKay, 1970.

Miller, J., and others. "Women and Work: The Psychological Effects of Occupational Conditions." *American Journal of Sociology*, 1979, *85*, 66–94.

Mizruchi, E. H. "Social Structure and Anomia in a Small City." *American Sociological Review*, 1960, *5*, 645–654.

Muthén, B. "A Structural Probit Model with Latent Variables." *Journal of the American Statistical Association*, 1979, *74*, 807–811.

Neal, A. G., and Rettig, S. "Dimensions of Alienation Among Manual and Non-Manual Workers." *American Sociological Review*, 1963, *28*, 599–608.

Neal, A. G., and Rettig, S. "On the Multi-dimensionality of Alienation." *American Sociological Review*, 1967, *32* (1), 54–64.

Neal, A. G., and Seeman, M. "Organizations and Powerlessness: A Test of the Mediation Hypothesis." *American Sociological Review*, 1964, *29*, 216–226.

Newton, R. R., Prensky, D., and Schuessler, K. "Form Effects in the Measurement of Feeling States." Unpublished manuscript, 1982.

Phillips, D. L., and Clancy, K. J. "Response Biases in Field Studies of Mental Illness." *American Sociological Review*, 1970, *35*, 503–515.

Phillips, D. L., and Segal, B. F. "Sexual Status and Psychiatric Symptoms." *American Sociological Review*, 1969, *34*, 58–72.

Pierce, R. C., and Clark, M. M. "Measurement of Morale in the Elderly." Unpublished manuscript, Langley-Porter Neuropsychiatric Institute, 1972.

Reiser, M. "Latent Trait Modelling of Attitude Items." In G. W. Bohrnstedt and E. F. Borgatta (Eds.), *Social Measurement: Current Issues.* Beverly Issues, Calif.: Sage, 1981.

Robinson, J., and Shaver, P. *Measures of Social Psychological Attitudes.* Ann Arbor: Institute for Social Research, University of Michigan, 1972.

Rosenberg, M. *Occupations and Values.* New York: Free Press, 1957.

Rosenberg, M. "The Dissonant Religious Context and Emotional Disturbance." *American Journal of Sociology*, 1962, *68*, 1–10.

Rotter, J. B. "Generalized Expectancies for Internal Versus External Control of Reinforcement." *Psychological Monographs*, 1966, *80*, 1–28.

Rundquist, E., and Sletto, R. *Personality in the Depression.* Minneapolis: University of Minnesota Press, 1936.

Schuessler, K. *Analyzing Social Data.* Boston: Houghton Mifflin, 1971.

Schuessler, K., and Freshnock, L. "Measuring Attitudes Toward Self and Others in Society: State of the Art." *Social Forces*, 1978, *56*, 1228–1244.

Schuessler, K., Hittle, D., and Cardascia, J. "Measuring Responding Desirably with Attitude-Opinion Items." *Social Psychology*, 1978, *41*, 224–235.

Schuessler, K., and Wallace, M. "Components in Communality of Mental Attitude Items." *Sociological Focus*, 1979, *12*, 247–261.

Schuman H., and Presser S. "The Assessment of 'No Opinion' in Attitude Surveys." In K. Schuessler (Ed.), *Sociological Methodology 1979.* San Francisco: Jossey-Bass, 1978.

Seeman, M. "On the Meaning of Alienation." *American Sociological Review*, 1959, *24*, 783-791.

Sheppard, H., and Herrick, N. *Where Have All the Robots Gone? Worker Dissatisfaction in the '70's*. New York: Free Press, 1972.

Singer, G. *Morale Factors in Industrial Management*. New York: Exposition Press, 1961.

Smith, D. H. "A Psychological Model of Individual Participation in Formal Voluntary Organizations: Application to Some Chilean Data." *American Journal of Sociology*, 1966, *72*, 249-266.

Srole, L. "Social Integration and Certain Corollaries: An Exploratory Study." *American Sociological Review*, 1956, *21*, 709-716.

Stevens, S. S. "Measurement, Psychophysics and Utility." In C. W. Churchman and P. Ratoosh (Eds.), *Measurement: Definition and Theories*. New York: Wiley, 1959.

Stouffer, S. A., and Lazarsfeld, P. F. *Research Memorandum on the Family in the Depression*. New York: Social Science Research Council, 1937.

Stouffer, S. A., and others. *Measurement and Prediction*. Princeton, N.J.: Princeton University Press, 1949.

Struening, E. L., and Richardson, A. H. "A Factor Analytic Exploration of the Alienation, Anomia, and Authoritarianism Domain." *American Sociological Review*, 1965, *30*, 768-776.

Thurstone, L. L., and Chave, E. J. *The Measurement of Attitude*. Chicago: University of Chicago Press, 1929.

Torgerson, W. S. *Theory and Methods of Scaling*. New York: Wiley, 1967.

Tucker, L., and Lewis, C. "A Reliability Coefficient for Maximum Likelihood Factor Analysis." *Psychometrika*, 1973, *38*, 1-10.

W. E. Upjohn Institute for Employment Research. *Work in America*. Cambridge, Mass.: M.I.T. Press, 1973.

U.S. Strategic Bombing Survey. *The Effects of Strategic Bombing on German Morale*. Washington, D.C.: U.S. Government Printing Office, 1947.

Van Dusen, R. A., and Zill, N. (Eds.). *Basic Background Items for U.S. Households Surveys*. Washington, D.C.: Social Science Research Council, 1975.

Walker, N. *Morale in the Civil Service.* Edinburgh: Edinburgh University Press, 1961.

Wheaton, B. "The Sociogenesis of Psychological Disorder: Reexamining the Causal Issues with Longitudinal Data." *American Sociological Review,* 1978, *43*, 383–403.

Zeller, R. A., Neal, A. G., and Groat, H. T. "On the Reliability & Stability of Alienation Measures: A Longitudinal Analysis." *Social Forces,* 1980, *58*, 1195–1204.

Index

A

Acquiescing scale (A16), 90–91, 94–95, 98–99, 102, 119–122; construction of, 105–106; reliability of, 107–108, 115–116, 120; use of, 116–119, 122; validity of, 108–114, 120–122

Affect balance scale, 6

Affect states. *See* Feelings; Social life feelings

Age, and response to SLFSs, 75–84, 111, 117. *See also* Older people

Agree-disagree items, scoring of, 12. *See also* Keyed responses

Aiken, M., 57, 158

Alienation tests, 2, 5, 8, 10. *See also* Morale; SLFS5; SLFS8

Alienation via rejection scale, 57–58

Alpha coefficient: calculation of, 163; of SLFSs, 14–15, 40

Alpha reliability: of response-set scales, 107–108; and scale criteria, 43–44; and scale length, 65; of SLFSs, 132

Always, sometimes, never responses, scoring of, 12. *See also* Keyed responses

American Journal of Sociology, 7, 53, 141

American Psychological Association, 109

American Sociological Review, 53, 141

Andrews, F. M., 10, 87

Annals of the American Academy of Political and Social Sciences, 7

Anomie, scales for, 5, 8–9, 56–58, 60

Answer categories. *See* Responses

Anxiety scale, 57

Apathy scales, 64

Apter, D. E., 168

Arminger, E., 44
Armor, D. J., 167
Author scales, 55–56; correlations
with SLFSs, 56–62, 70, 138–139;
means and standard deviations
for, 158

B

Black college students, measures of
control of, 5–6. *See also* Race
"Black Ghetto Diversity and Ano-
mie" (Kapsis), 138
Block, J., 88
Bohrnstedt, G. W., 163, 169, 172
Borgatta, E. F., 169, 172
Bradburn, N., 6, 10, 38–39, 57–59,
62, 64–65, 141, 158
British civil service, job satisfaction
scale, 59
Buckland, W. R., 163–164
Butler, S., 8

C

Caplovitz, D., 6, 38–39, 57–58, 62,
64–65, 141
Cardascia, J., 104
Career Concerns scale. *See* SLFS12
Carmines, E. G., 163
Carr, L. E., 112
Carroll, J. B., 44, 162
Cartwright, D. S., 5
Categorical judgement scales, 3
Cavan, R., 8, 57
Chave, E. J., 136
Cherline, A., 6
Child, I. L., 7
Churchman, C. W., 173
Citizen involvement scale, 59. *See
also* SLFS5; SLFS8
Clancy, K. J., 116
Clark, M. M., 57
Class means: PEV of, 75; responses
to SLFSs and, 75–81; scale rank-
ing by, 81–82
Cleary, P. D., 138
Coefficients: calculation of, 161–
165; choice of, 44–45
Combat duty, and scale develop-
ment, 7–8, 10

Comrey, A. L., 168
Concepts: defining of and item
choice, 13; differentiation of, 2–7.
See also Content domains; Items
Concordance coefficient, 163–164
Conklin, J. E., 57
Content domains: development of,
9–10, 141–143; and item choice,
11; and scale construction, 53–54;
of SLFSs and sources, 56
Control: internal/external (scale),
5–6, 57, 62; measures of, 5–6; per-
sonal (scale), 57. *See also* SLFS1
Converse, P. E., 2
Correlations: of first-factor scores,
15; interscale, 48-50; of item to-
tals, 14; mean interitem, 14–15,
46
Costner, H., 167
Crandall, D. L., 168
Crowne, D. P., 89, 91, 100–101, 106–
107, 148, 151
Cumming, E., 57, 141, 158
Cynicism, about government and
politics. *See* SLFS5; SLFS8;
about people. *See* SLFS2; SLFS7

D

Dean, D., 5
Dean, L. R., 57, 158
Dejection, scales of, 64
Democracy, faith in. *See* SLFS5
Demographic factors. *See* Age; Edu-
cation; Income; Marital state;
Race; Sex
Demoralization feelings. *See* SLFS11
Depression, and scale development,
6–7
Depression measures. *See* SLFS3
Depressive affect scale, 57, 59
Despair scales. *See* SLFS11
Dichotomous indicators, 137
Disenchantment, 7, 10. *See also*
Morale
Disillusionment: with government.
See SLFS8; with people. *See*
SLFS7
Dissatisfaction. *See* Alienation; Job
dissatisfaction

Disturbance terms, 43
Dodder, R. A., 5
Dohrenwend, B. P., 57, 104, 116
Dohrenwend, B. S., 104, 116
Doubt about Self-Determination
    scale. See SLFS1
Doubt about Trustworthiness of
    People scale. See SLFS2
Down Feelings scale. See SLFS3
Duncan, O. D., 137

E

Economic Self-Determination scale.
    See SLFS10
Education, and responses to SLFSs,
    75-84, 111, 117
Edwards, A. L., 88
Efficacy in public affairs scale, 57,
    59
Eigenvalues: of items, 47; of SLFSs,
    14-15
Élan, scales of, 64
Equal-appearing intervals, 3, 136

F

Factor analysis, 44, 46, 138; model
    of, 164
Factor loading, 14; of items, 46-47,
    49-53; of SLFSs, 14-39
Faith in Citizen Involvement scale.
    See SLFS5
Faith in People scale. See SLFS2
Fears, items on, 46
Feeling Demoralized scale, See
    SLFS11
Feeling Down scale. See SLFS3
Feeling Up scale. See SLFS6
Feelings: about self. See SLFS1;
    SLFS3; SLFS4; SLFS6; SLFS10;
    about society. See SLFS2; SLFS5;
    SLFS7; SLFS8; SLFS9; positive
    and negative, 12
Ferman, L., 57
Finney, D. J., 137
First factor scores; correlations of for
    SLFSs, 15
Freshnock, L., 2
Future Outlook scale, See SLFS9

G

Geerken, M. R., 116
Gove, W. R., 116
Government, disillusionment with.
    See SLFS5; SLFS8; participation
    scales, 59
Greene, V. L., 163
Groat, H. T., 57, 138
Gurin, E., 138
Gurin, P., 3, 5, 57, 61-62, 138
Guttman, L., 3, 136
Guttman reproducibility, 15
Guttman scales, 3, 136

H

Hadaway, C., 138
Harman, H. H., 138, 164
Heise, D. R., 163
Herrick, N., 8, 57
Hittle, D., 104
Horst, P., 162, 169

I

Idealism, and cynicism scales, 30
Income, and responses to SLFSs, 75-
    84, 111, 117
Individual and government scales.
    See SLFS5
Individualism, and alienation, 58
Interitem correlations, 14-15, 46, 48
Internal/external control scale, 5-6,
    57, 62
Interscale correlations, 48-50
Interviewing, 152-154
Involvement, of citizens. See SLFS5
Isolation feelings. See SLFS3
Isolation scale, 57
Item-total correlates, 14-39
Items: on background characteris-
    tics, 151; choice of, 4, 10, 11-12;
    clusters of, and class means, 83;
    differentiation of, 2-3; factoring
    of, 50-54; homogeneity within
    scales of, 45-46; meaningfulness
    of, 133-134; on more than one
    scale, 9, 14-39, 48-52; screening

Items (continued)
  and selection of, 13, 42, 46–48,
  142–143; semantic specificity of,
  2–3; sources of, 56–57, 141–143;
  wording and subject classification of, 71–72

J

Jackman, M. R., 57
Jackson, D. N., 89, 91, 96–99, 102–
  103, 148, 151
Jackson-Messick Acquiescing scale
  (JMA10), 91, 98–99, 151; con-
  struction of, 102–103; reliability
  of, 107–108, 115; validity of,
  108–114
Jackson Responding Desirably scale
  (JRD10), 91, 96–97, 151; con-
  struction of, 102–103; reliability
  of, 107–108, 115–116; validity of,
  108–114
Job morale scales, 57, 59
Job satisfaction scale. See SLFS4
Jöreskog, K. G., 133, 136
Journals, as source of items, 141

K

Kalleberg, A. L., 138
Kapsis, R. E., 138
Kendall, M. G., 163–164
Kessler, R. C., 138
Key, reversing of and correlations,
  12
Key-balancing, of topic scales, 63
Key-uniform scales, 14
Keyed responses, 14–39
Kim, J., 162
Kohn, M. L., 57, 138

L

Langner, T. S., 57, 158
Latent structure models, 136
Latent variables, relation to prior
  causes, 136–137
Lawley, D. N., 164
Lazarsfeld, P. F., 7, 136
Leggett, J. C., 112

Lenski, G. E., 112
Levonian, E., 168
Lewis, C., 4, 164–165
"Life Satisfaction and Religion: A
  Reanalysis" (Hadaway), 138
Likert, R., 3, 136
Lingoes, J. C., 138
LISREL model, 136–137
Loadings, factor (varimax), 14, 46–
  47, 49–53
Lord, F. M., 137, 163
Lowenthal, M. F., 8
Lystad, M. H., 171

M

Marital status, and responses to
  SLFSs, 75–84, 111
Marlowe, D., 89, 91, 100–101, 106–
  107, 148, 151
Marlowe-Crowne Social Desirabil-
  ity scale (MCSD10) 91, 100–101,
  151; construction of, 106–107; re-
  liability of, 107–108, 115; validity
  of, 108–114, 120
Martin, E., 169
Marx, G., 57
Maxwell, E. A., 164
McClosky, H., 57, 69–70
Mead, M., 133
Mean: of SLFSs, 14–39
Mean correlations: interitem, 14–15;
  of items within scales, 43
Meaning: and item usefulness, 71–
  72; nonresponding as test of,
  133–134. See also concepts; Se-
  mantic issues
Meaninglessness scale, 57
Median, of SLFSs, 14–39
Mental illness, measures of, 9–10
Messick, S., 88–89, 91, 98–99, 102–
  103, 108, 148, 151
Miller, D. C., 142
Miller, J., 137
Minnesota Multiphasic Personality
  Test, and social desirability
  scales, 102, 119
Missing responses rate, 12–13; by
  questionnaire section, 159; as

validity measure, 133–134; value estimation for, 158–160
Mizruchi, E. H., 57
Morale: of older people, 36; scales for, 57; tests of, 2, 7–8, 10; of workers. *See* SLFS4. *See also* Alienation; Feelings
Morrison, B. M., 138
Muthén, B., 86, 137

N

National Survey Questionnaire: administration of, 147–151; sample means of, 14–39; sampling and interviewing on, 152–154. *See also* Items; Questionnaire; Scales; Social Life Feeling Scales
Neal, A. G., 5, 57, 138, 158
Negative feelings, 12; scale for, 57–58
Negative statements, response-set for, 26. *See also* Aquiescing Scale; Responding Desirably scale
Newell, D. S., 57
Newton, R. R., 150
Normlessness, 7; measures of, 9. *See also* Morale
Novick, M. R., 137, 163

O

"Occupational Structure and Alienation" (Kohn), 138
Older people, morale scales for, 8, 36. *See also* Retired persons; SLFS11
One-factor model, 43
Opinion polling, and mental measurement, 9–10
Optimism scale. *See* SLFS11

P

Paired comparisons, 3
People: cynicism about (scale). *See* SLFS7; faith in (scales), 57–58; trustworthiness of (scale). *See* SLFS2

Percentage explained variance (PEV), 73–74; and class means, 74–81; frequency of rank for background factors, 82, 85–86; frequency of rank for clusters, 83–84
Personal control scale, 57, 62
Personal efficacy scale, 57
Personality inventories, as item sources, 142
Personality items, 108
Personality Research Form, 102
Pessimism about social life. *See* SLFS9
Phi coefficient, 44–45; calculation of, 161–162; class frequencies of, 45–46
Phillips, D. L., 116
Pierce, R. C., 57
Pilot study, 144–147
Point biserial correlation, 14; calculation of, 162–163
Political democracy scale. *See* SLFS5
Politicians, cynicism about. *See* SLFS5; SLFS8
Populations: defined for SLFSs, 152; and acale proliferation, 2–4, 9. *See also* Social factors
Positive feeling, 12; scale of, 57
Positive statements, response-sets of, 26
Positive thinking scale, 57
Powerlessness scale, 57
Prensky, D., 150
Presser, S., 147
Product-moment correlations, 14; and item selection, 42; and scale definition, 44
Psychological symptom index, 57, 59
Public affairs, efficacy scales, 57, 59, 60
Public opinion polls, and confidence measures, 9
Purposelessness scale, 57, 60

Q

Questionnaire: administration of, 147–151; construction of, 14; pre-

Questionnaire (continued)
  tests of, 150. *See also* Items;
  National Survey Questionnaire;
  Scoring; Social Life Feeling
  Scales

R

Rabjohn, J., 162
Race, and responses to SLFSs, 75–84, 111, 117
Ratio estimation scales, 3
Ratoosh, P., 173
Reeder, L. G., 6
Reiser, M., 137
Reliability: and length of scale, 40, 65. *See also* Alpha reliability; Tucker-Lewis reliability coefficient
Reproducibility. *See* Guttman reproducibility
Responding Desirably scale (RD16), 90–93, 96–97, 119–122; construction of, 103; item correlations of, 113–114; reliability of, 107–108, 115–116; uses of, 116–119, 122; validity of, 108–114, 120–121
Response Analysis Inc., 148, 150, 152–153, 155
Response-set scales: relation of SLFSs to, 114–116; reliability of, 107–108; validity of, 108–114
Response sets, 88; items for measuring of, 148; and SLFS scores, 89
Responses: agree and disagree, 12; in scale construction, 53–54; scoring, 42. *See also* Missing responses rate
Retired persons, and scale development, 8, 10
Rettig, S., 5
Richardson, A. H., 5, 57, 60–61
Robinson, J., 56
Rosenberg, M., 13, 57–59
Rotter, J. B., 3, 5–6, 57, 62
Rundquist, E., 7, 57, 61, 141

S

Sampling, 6, 152–154; weighting of, 155–158

Satisfaction scale, 57
Scales: clustering of, 49–50; constructing of, 42, 53–54; criteria for, 43–44; homogeneity of items within, 45–46; interpretation basis for, 13; item selection for, 46–48; key-balanced or key-uniform, 14; length considerations, 40; length of and reliability, 65; marginals for items of, 156–157; reliability considerations, 40; search for in literature, 142; social issues in construction of, 6–10. *See also* Items; Questionnaire; Social Life Feeling Scales
Scaling: developments in, 2–4; by equal-appearing intervals, 72; trends in methodology of, 2–4, 136–137
Scalogram analysis, 138
Schaar, J. H., 57, 69–70
Schooler, C., 57
Schuman, H., 121, 147
Scores: of tests and factors correlated, 15
Scoring: of negative and positive items, 12; of pilot survey, 146–147; and response sets, 89. *See also* Missing responses rate
Seeman, M., 3, 57
Segal, B. F., 116
Self and government. *See* SLFS5
Self-determination, doubts about. *See* SLFS1
Self determination, economic. *See* SLFS10
Self-feelings scales. *See* SLFS1; SLFS3; SLFS4; SLFS6; SLFS10
Selfishness of people. *See* SLFS7
Semantic issues, 2–3. *See also* Content domains; Items; Meaning; Subject scales
Sex, and SDVS, 104, 111
Shaver, P., 56
Sheppard, H., 8, 57
Simplex scales, 3, 136
Singer, G., 173
Sletto, R., 7, 57, 61, 141, 158

Smith, D. H., 57, 59
Social class, and response set,
   110-114
"Social Class and Psychological
   Distress" (Kessler and Cleary),
   138
Social desirability scale 91, 100-101;
   item scaling on, 103. *See also*
   Jackson Responding Desirably
   scale; Marlowe-Crowne Social
   Desirability scale
Social desirability scale values
   (SDSVs): constructing of, 103-
   105; item correlations of, 113-
   114; item selection on, 104-105
Social factors, and responses to
   questionnaires. *See* Age; Education; Income; Marital status;
   Race; Sex
Social Forces, 53, 141
Social isolation scales, 57
Social life, trends. *See* SLFS9
Social life feelings, 1, 11; measurement literature, 3-6; measurement practice, 1930-1970, 1-4;
   research operations in measuring
   of, 4-5
Social Life Feeling Scales (SLFSs);
   author scale correlations of, 55-
   62; background factors and research designs of, 84-86; best
   item-total correlations, closest
   scales of, 124-127; class means
   and PEVs for, 75; factor loadings
   for, 50-53; interpretation of, 128-
   131, 135; interscale correlations
   of, 157-158; origins of, 3-4, 6-10;
   pilot survey for, 144-147; reliability and dimensionality of,
   132-135; and response-set scales,
   114-116; sampling and interviewing for, 152-154; subject
   classes of, 65-68, 71; summary
   ratings of, 134-136; topic scale
   correlations of, 62-65, 70-71;
   validity of, 131-132. *See also*
   Items; Questionnaire, Scaling;
   Scoring
SLFS1 (Doubt About Self-Determination), 15-17, 124; class means

for, 76; correlations with author
   scales, 56-58; correlations with
   SLFS6, 116-117; correlations
   with topic scales, 63; subject
   classes of, 66, 68; validity of, 128,
   132
SLFS2 (Doubt About Trustworthiness of People), 15, 18-19, 124;
   class means for, 76-77; correlations with author scales of, 58;
   correlations with topic scales of,
   63-64; interpretation of, 13; subject class of, 66; validity of,
   128-129
SLFS3 (Feeling Down), 15, 20-22,
   26, 124-125; class means for, 77;
   correlations with author scales
   of, 58-59; correlations with topic
   scales of, 64; subject class of, 66;
   validity of, 129
SLFS4 (Job Satisfaction), 15, 22-23,
   125; class means for, 77; correlations with author scales of, 59;
   correlations with topic scales of,
   63-64; subject classes of, 66-67;
   validity of, 129
SLFS5 (Faith in Citizen Involvement), 15, 24-25, 30, 125; class
   means for, 78; correlations with
   author scales of, 59; correlations
   with topic scales of, 63-64; subject classes of, 67; validity of,
   129-130
SLFS6 (Feeling Up), 15, 26-27, 125-
   126; class means for, 78; correlations with author scales of, 59-60;
   correlations with SLFS1, 116-
   117; subject classes of, 67; validity
   of, 130
SLFS7 (People Cynicism), 15, 28-
   29, 126; class means for, 78-79;
   correlations with author scales
   of, 60; correlations with topic
   scales of, 64; subject classes of,
   67-68; validity of, 130
SLFS8 (Disillusionment with Government), 15, 30-31, 126; class
   means for, 79; correlations with
   author scales of, 60-61; correla-

SLFS8 (continued)
  tions with topic scales of, 63–64;
  subject classes of, 67; validity of,
  130
SLFS9 (Future Outlook), 15, 32–33,
  126–127; class means of, 79–80;
  correlation with author scales of,
  61; correlations with topic scales
  of, 64; subject classes of, 67; validity of, 130
SLFS10 (Economic Self-Determination), 15, 34–35, 127; class means
  for, 80; correlations with author
  scales of, 61; correlations with
  topic scales of, 63; subject classes
  of, 67–68; validity of, 130–131
SLFS11 (Feeling Demoralized), 15,
  36–37, 127; class means of, 80;
  correlations with author scales
  of, 61–62; correlations with topic
  scales of, 63; subject classes of,
  67–68; validity of, 131
SLFS12 (Career Concerns), 15, 38–
  39, 48, 127; class means of, 81;
  correlations with author scales
  of, 62; correlations with topic
  scales of, 64–65; subject classes of,
  68; validity of, 131
Social means, and response-set measures, 110–114
Social problems, and social life feel-
  ings measurement, 6–10
Social psychiatry, and scale development, 3–4, 9
Social Psychology Quarterly, 53, 141
Social relevance issues, and reliabil-
  ity measures, 40–41
Social sciences, specialization trends
  in, 3–4
Social Trust scale. *See* SLFS2
Society, feelings about. *See* SLFS2;
  SLFS5; SLFS7; SLFS8; SLFS9
Sociometry, 53, 141
Sörbom, D., 133, 136
Spearman two-factor model, 43
Srole, L., 5, 55–58, 60, 128, 158
Standard deviations, of SLFSs, 14–
  39
*Standards for Educational and Psy-
  chological Tests*, 109

Stevens, S. S., 3, 86
Stouffer, S. A., 7, 170
Struening, E. L., 5, 57, 60–61, 158
Subject scales, correlations with
  SLFSs, 65–68, 71. *See also* Scales;
  Scaling

T

Tests, proliferation of, 3–4. *See also*
  Items; Questionnaire; Scaling;
  Scoring; Social Life Feeling
  Scales
Tetrachoric correlation coefficient:
  interitem, 44–45; calculation of,
  162
Thurstone, L. L., 3, 136
Topic scales, 55; correlations with
  SLFSs, 62–65, 70–71; key -
  uniform, 63
Torgerson, W. S., 137
Trust, social. *See* SLFS2
Trustworthiness of People scale. *See*
  SLFS2
Tucker, L., 4, 164–165
Tucker-Lewis reliability coefficient
  (TLRC): calculation of, 164–165;
  and item selection, 4–5, 43–44,
  47; and phi coefficient, 45–46;
  and scale length, 65; of SLFSs,
  14–15, 40; as validity measure,
  132–135
Turner, C. F., 169

U

Unemployment, and morale tests
  development, 7, 10
Up feelings. *See* SLFS6
Upjohn Institute for Employment
  Research, 8
U.S. Strategic Bombing Survey, 7–8
Usefulness, scales of, 57

V

Van Dusen, R. A., 148
Varimax loadings, 14, 46–47, 49–53

W

Walker, N., 57, 59
Wallace, M., 65

Well-being scales, 59
Wheaton, B., 174
Withey, S. B., 10, 87
Women, alienation study of, 5
"Work Values and Job Rewards"
  (Kalleberg), 138
Worker morale tests, 8. *See also*
  SLFS4

World War II, and scale develop-
  ment, 7–8
Worries scales, 38, 40, 57. *See also*
  SLFS12

Z

Zeller, R. A., 138
Zill, N., 148

DATE DUE

Alison Yohno	
IL 04 88	
12-11-24	
FEB 0 8 '89	

BRODART, INC. Cat. No. 23-221